Werner Blaser

**Mies van der Rohe
Continuing the Chicago School
of Architecture**

Second edition

1981
Birkhäuser Verlag
Basel · Boston · Stuttgart

First published under the title
Mies van der Rohe:
Principles and School/Lehre und Schule
Edited by the Institute for the History and
Theory of Architecture at the Swiss Federal
Institute of Technology, Zurich
in the book series *Exploration (Vol. 3).*
(Birkhäuser Verlag) Basel und Stuttgart, 1977

Library of Congress Cataloging in Publication Data

Blaser, Werner, 1924–
    Mies van der Rohe, continuing the Chicago
school of architecture.
    Expanded translation of: Mies van der Rohe,
Lehre und Schule.
      Bibliography: p.
      Included index.
      1. Mies van der Rohe, Ludwig, 1886–1969.
2. Architecture – Philosophy. I. Title.
NA 1088.M65B5813   1981   720'.92'4   81-12300
ISBN 3-7643-1247-5   AACR2

CIP-Kurztitelaufnahme der Deutschen Bibliothek

Blaser, Werner:
Mies van der Rohe: continuing the Chicago School
of Architecture/Werner Blaser. – 2. ed. –
Basel; Boston; Stuttgart: Birkhäuser, 1981.
    ISBN 3-7643-1247-5
NE: Mies van der Rohe, Ludwig [III.]

© 1981 Birkhäuser Verlag Basel
Layout: Werner Blaser, Albert Gomm
Printed in Switzerland by Birkhäuser AG,
Graphisches Unternehmen, Basel
ISBN 3-7643-1247-5

Contents

3

Introduction

My first book on Mies van der Rohe 'The Art of
Structure' was published in Chicago in 1963-64. I
had been authorized by Mies to undertake the
work and it was produced with his cooperation.
Now that Mies has been dead for eight years, I
want to show in this publication the principles on
which he created his work and established his
teaching, and also how his successors are continuing to work on this basis. Sharing their thinking has
been of great value to me in this task. Obviously
the educational program of the Department of Architecture of IIT (Illinois Institute of Technology,
Chicago) should occupy a prominent position in
these pages. It embraces all the essential principles
on which Mies and his students worked and later
realized their designs. By making available com-
prehensive source material and describing its
method of teaching and its buildings, I hope to
show the school of Mies in a way that will be an in-
spiration to architects and mark out a future line of
advance. Although the influence of the school of
Mies and its teaching has been worldwide, I must
concentrate mainly on the region of Chicago and on
the alumni of IIT so that I can present the school of
Mies against the background of its most immediate
outgrowth. Today a number of ex-students are
working as faculty at IIT and at the same time as
independent architects or partners in large offices
in Chicago. The purpose of my work is to crystal-
lize the educational work of Mies and more particularly the essential ideas that permeate his school
and have found many adherents, and to present an
account of what the school does in words and pictures with a clarity and simplicity that would be
consistent with Mies' own attitude. The book will
present Mies' educational work as head of the
Department of Architecture at IIT in Chicago from
1938 to 1958 and the work of his successors as architects and teachers (1959-75, under George
E. Danforth and since 1975 under James Ingo
Freed) down to 1977. The book thus falls into three
parts – principles – master – successors or in other
words, teaching at IIT, works by Mies in Chicago
1939-69, buildings by his followers and their activities at IIT.

The principles of Mies

Teaching implies the mediation of knowledge
through a theoretical presentation of a branch of
learning and through the practical application of
the material taught. Theory and realization call for
rules and a logical structure. These form the essential basis of teaching and learning. Mies gave his
mind to the practical training of architects while
still in Europe, at the Bauhaus at Dessau and Berlin in 1930–33, and wrote down his ideas. His introductory address as head of the Department of Architecture at Armour Institute of Technology in
Chicago (AIT, later IIT) – testimonial dinner
speech at Palmer House on November 20, 1938 –
was, I have found, quite definitely composed in
Germany (p. 28–30). The original of this speech
was in a box which did not reach Chicago until
1964 along with the residue of his Berlin office.
Comparison of this original text with a copy that
was made later in the States with an American
typewriter proved to me that the address was formulated in Germany. Mies' educational work in
America could thus be established on principles
which had already assumed their basic form on European soil. When Mies came to the Bauhaus at
Dessau in 1930 the basic principles of what he
taught were already apparent in his buildings and
consequently his students could apply these principles in their work. The courtyard house project of
the American student Howard Dearstyne (p. 12–13),
developed during the Bauhaus period in Dessau,
shows a spatial design with brick walls enclosing
the house and courtyard: space is primary and the
position of the walls is determined by it. Interior
and exterior form a whole. In this spatial freedom
the static principle of slab, beam and column, i.e.
of load and support, can be expressed. As the logical sequel to these lucid requirements we have the
articulation of proportions in surface and space.
Playful fancy is replaced by a clear system of structure on which Mies had already worked for
decades in Germany. Precisely the example of the
courtyard house has been applied with particular
success by students in their studies at IIT down to
the present day. Free as it is from excessively narrow functional constraints, it is an exercise in which
the principles of systematic architecture can be
studied clearly and concretely: the essential nature
of the brick wall, the non-load-bearing inner walls,
the determination of the structure in space, the arrangement of the furniture, and the integration
with painting and sculpture.
The curriculum gives the student at IIT the knowledge and skill indispensable for his profession, i.e.
a fundamental training which enables him to utilize his ability. During the first semester the emphasis is placed on drawing and at the same time
visual imagination is fostered. In the second year
simple structures of brick, wood and stone are
practised. These are followed by studies of mass
and proportion. The third year teaches the student
to analyze and present a simple dwelling house in
7

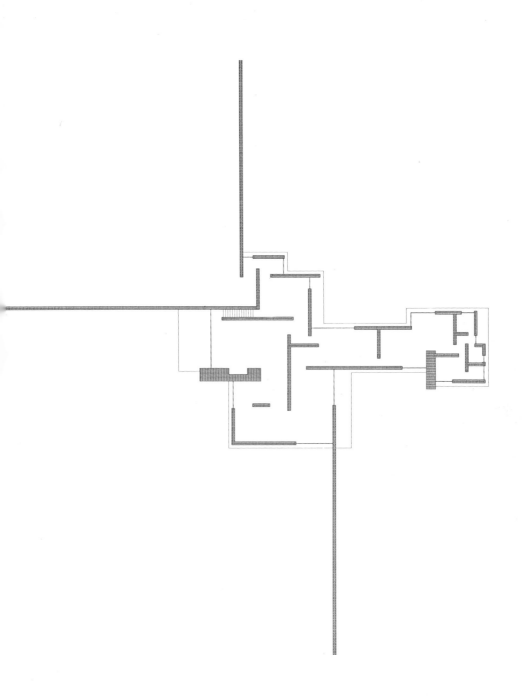

Brick country house project by Mies 1923
(drawing from 1964).
9

terms of its function. One theme is the study of concrete and steel structures. In the fourth year follows the study of more complex problems with reference to appropriate buildings and also an introduction to city planning. In the fifth year, the last before graduation, the student may choose between concentrated studies in architecture or city planning. During the whole five years mathematics, structural statics, and the arts are taught. The study of the history of architecture is also important. The student should understand the principles underlying the various types and methods of building of past epochs. What is involved here is an understanding of architecture at a more profound level and not merely imitation. Through his awareness of the cultural situations of the past the student will learn to understand and interpret the present with greater clarity.

In the IIT Bulletin for the Graduate Courses 1944–45 appeared for the first time the five principles of architecture formulated by Mies and constituting (IIT Bulletin after 1949–50) the material for the last two years of undergraduate study. They are:

1. The structure as an architectural factor: its possibilities and limitations.
2. Space as an architectural problem.
3. Proportion as a means of architectural expression.
4. The expression value of materials.
5. Painting and sculpture in their relationship to architecture.

The application of these principles.

Teaching began after 1946 in 'Alumni Memorial Hall' at IIT, and continued later in 'Crown Hall'. Thus the students had direct and immediate experience of how a glass and steel building is realized. Theory and practice were side by side. For a score of years Mies worked at IIT, not so much as a lecturer but rather as the master who spelled out the problems at the drawing board with his pupils and helped to solve them. He wrote very little by way of theory since he was more concerned with stating the problem in precise terms than with theoretical speculations. For him it was all a question of the practical problem, of working things out in detail. This explains, for example, the importance attached to drawing. Only the best was good enough. Mies once said to me: 'If I have to draw a straight line, I draw it as straight as I can. If I hammer in a nail, I don't hit my fingers.' These words are also the key to one of the secrets of Mies' influence on his students. A recently discovered diagram 'Program for architectural education' of 1937 (p. 25–27), Mies' first draft of the curriculum for IIT, was based on the following fundamental questions of architectural education: from the study of the materials with which one builds and the analysis of the purposes for which one builds to reflections on the theme of architecture as art. Two prominent personalities had, like Mies, come from the Bauhaus in Dessau and Berlin; these were the mathematician and photographer Walter Peter-

10

hans for visual training, and the architect and planner Ludwig Hilberseimer for city planning. They gave him their help and transferred his ideas to their fields of teaching at IIT from the very outset. At IIT Mies worked with his students to develop projects in terms of the principles involved before any opportunity for execution offered itself. One of the essential preliminaries to planning a building is a close study of the building material and its applicability. This can be done, for example, by means of collages. The structure is always tested for its possibilities and limitations when it is separated into skin and skeleton. The relationships between space and proportion are studied with reference to the model. These subjects of student studies range from the dwelling house to the public building and the city, from the small room to the spacious hall. This development takes place through the medium of visual training (photomontages and collages), at the drawing board, and in the workshop.

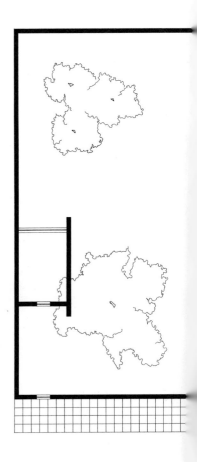

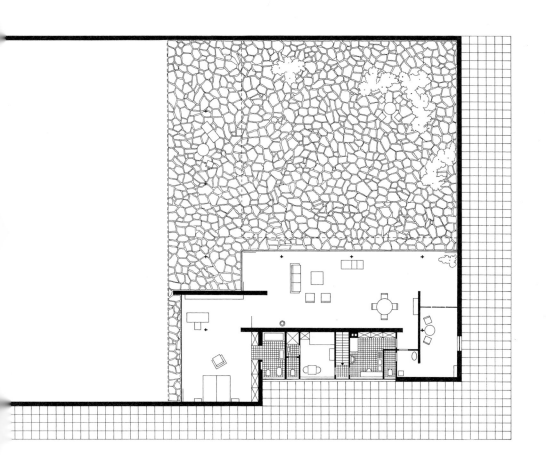

Plan of a courtyard house by Howard Dearstyne,
Bauhaus (under Mies) Dessau, 1931 (scale 1:300).

13

The school of Mies

In Latin the word 'schola' was transferred to the
followers of a teacher. In this sense the concept still
survives as a name for a movement which bears the
impress of a personality. In summary the school of
Mies is understood to mean a conception of work
as a form of structural expression within which
many variations are possible. The constant progress
in technical achievements allows successors to venture on modifications without deviating from what
is essential. That is the strength of the school of
Mies: once a principle has been elaborated it is adhered to and varied over many years. We find the
fundamental laws of space and structure realized
down to the smallest detail.
As everyone knows, the first skyscrapers were built
in Chicago in the eighties and nineties of the
19th century using the steel skeleton. Shortly after
his arrival in Chicago Mies said: 'The most important idea in modern architecture is the idea of the
skeleton building developed here in Chicago.'
Leading architects such as Jenney, Burnham, Root
and Sullivan initiated a development which came
to be called the 'Chicago School of Architecture'.
Starting to work in Chicago half a century later,
Mies van der Rohe continued this tradition. In this
way the 'Second School of Architecture' was
begun. Mies continued the tradition of the Chicago
School as a heritage which placed him under an
obligation. He once said: 'The purpose the building serves is constantly changing but we cannot afford to demolish it. And so we turn Sullivan's slo-
gan on its head and build a convenient and economical space into which we fit function and in
which it can change.' This principle can be recog-
nized as far back as the brick country house project
of 1923. He conceived the rooms as a continuum;
there are, as it were, no dividing lines between interior and exterior. Mies first jotted down the idea
of this brick villa in a charcoal drawing.
Some forty years later I drew the positions of the
bricks exactly to scale (p. 8–9). It is characteristic of
Mies that he preferred the word 'development' to
'design'. Mies said: 'We do not produce designs.
We consider what might be done and then we try
to develop it, and then we accept it. We always
develop in accordance with critical criteria.' Further, Mies preferred to speak of 'Baukunst' (building art) rather than of 'Architektur'. 'Bau' is the
structure and 'Kunst' is the creative design. Starting
with a spatial concept Mies always deployed his
ideas on the basis of a clear construction, i.e. a regular construction in which the dimensional
modules are varied repeatedly or in an ordered
manner. The important thing is that the construction should form a logical whole. Construction is
the name for the way in which building elements
and building materials are joined together. Structure on the other hand is the name for the structural organization of a building and its basis in statics. Mies said in 1965: 'I brought clarity, reason and
modern means to architecture and opened up
14

space. I developed construction and illustrated it in a variety of buildings.' And on another occasion later in the same year: 'When clear construction is elevated to an exact expression, that is what I call architecture.'

This philosophy can be connected with that of Viollet-Le-Duc, whom he esteemed highly. For Viollet-Le-Duc architecture was the fulfilment of the purpose of a building with the technical means and methods of the age. To be true, for him, meant the fulfilment of all the requirements of purpose. For him artistic form was not, as it was for many of his contemporaries, something freely invented but the result of an ordered construction: 'Toute forme, qui n'est pas ordonnée par la structure, doit être repoussée.'

Rectangularity and the visualization of the skeleton as a means of order and as a basis for architectural design are among the characteristic elements of Mies' architecture. The clear distinction between 'skin' and 'skeleton' induced the Dutch painter Theo van Doesburg, who corresponded with Mies, to call him an anatomical architect. In the architecture of load-bearing and infilling Mies saw an analogy with man in that his physiology changes but his skeleton remains the same. In the external skin, the glass 'curtain wall', the creative inventiveness of the artist is particularly apparent. Structural clarity as the foundation of architecture remains the guiding principle for the school of Mies. Mies decided in favor of basic solutions to the problems of construction so as to leave his followers with scope for variations. He referred them to the examples of the classical works of Greek architecture and the order informing them. The basic principles are unique but there are untold variations. The same holds true of architectural design today. For a building Mies demanded the objective character of the construction in the largest possible number of variations.

The integration of space and art exemplified by a
Max Ernst Exhibition in the Art Institute of Chicago, November 1974. The logicality with which the
school of Mies places walls and exposes columns is
demonstrated in this exhibition room by James
Speyer.

17

The personality of Mies van der Rohe

The personality of Mies should not be given undue
prominence; yet the man Mies is inseparable from
his work and the principles he stood for in his
teaching. The mental world he inhabited might be
characterized by the books which influenced his
thinking and the works of art that surrounded him
in his home and stimulated his mind. In his apartment on East Pearson Street he always had within
handy reach books on St. Augustine, Lao-tse,
Buytendijk ('Erziehung zur Demut') and by the
philosopher Hartmann and the physicist Schroe-
dinger. On the walls hung, not as might be expect-
ed, works by Piet Mondrian, whom he held in very
high esteem, but pictures by Paul Klee and collages
by Kurt Schwitters. This casts an interesting light
on the man Mies and what he taught: it was not
pictorial geometry that interested him but the
imaginative, fanciful, and inventive, and
everything that reflected life in all its profusion.
That was his world, his home. It also included his
interest in the work of the craftsman with which he
became acquainted as an apprentice stone mason
in his father's business and later as a furniture
draughtsman with Bruno Paul. This explains his
profound concern with detail; for example, with
the ever-recurring problem of corners in a building, and his precise knowledge of materials. His
creations and the principles he taught are marked
by the unity of his mind and his work. Mies preferred to do his work in the seclusion of thought –
his kind of thought. 'I want to test my thinking in
doing,' he once said, 'I want to do something so
that I can think. Feeling also ought to be regulated
by doing.' Mies' work is penetrated by the 'adae-
quatio rei et intellectus' of his teacher Thomas
Aquinas. Thinking truly commensurate to its object – which would be our interpretation of adae-
quatio today – must make doing a rigorous ordering activity. 'Order is the meaning of the relationship between things,' said Mies. And where this
meaning is grasped in all its implications beauty
appears as the splendor of truth, as Mies taught us
in the words of St. Augustine. It was always
Mies' habit to express himself very tersely. He said
to me: 'When I read, I usually read the same text
several times and make notes. I read so intensively
that I cannot remember how my notes came to be
written because I was more concerned with the
meaning of the matter.' In another connection he
once said concerning building: 'I think that the influence my work has on other people is due to its
reasonableness. Everyone can work on it without
becoming an imitator because the work itself is objective from top to bottom. I think that if I myself
found something objective, I should make use of it.
It is of no consequence from whom it comes.' Mies'
working life covered five decades from 1918 to
1968. During this time he developed five types of
work in which principles of conception and construction are exemplified: all-glass towers with a
prismatic or polygonal plan (projects 1919–21, Ber-

18

lin), open-plan houses with steel columns (Barcelona Pavilion, 1929), all-glass houses with a steel frame (Farnsworth House at Plano, 1945–50), apartment and office towers with a steel frame and glass curtain wall (860–880 Lake Shore Drive Apartments in Chicago, 1948–51, and Seagram Building in New York, 1954–58), and steel-framed buildings with a wide roof span (Crown Hall on the IIT campus, 1950–56, Convention Hall in Chicago, 1953–54, New National Gallery in Berlin, 1962–68).

Mies' quest over many years for ultimate clarity of construction and his avoidance of any formal speculation – a process that began in Germany – found a favorable basis in the state of technology in the United States. The earlier buildings, expensive but perfect in their craftsmanship (such as the Barcelona Pavilion), were followed by the campus buildings in Chicago: low-cost inexpensive classroom buildings of Illinois Institute of Technology. Mies never built anything new for the sake of novelty; his plans and his technology arose from the essential quality and the purpose of the individual building. Also, he conceived any building he designed primarily as a unit and not just as a juxtaposition of rooms under a roof. In the matter of simplicity of construction and refinement of detail, Mies' influence extended far beyond Chicago and reached Europe. Mies' efforts to work along with the demands of technology led him to use modern materials economically and in accordance with their purpose and to bring out their beauty by rational use.

After 1938 Mies' activities at AIT were centered on the Art Institute of Chicago. James Speyer and George Danforth (right) worked on the courtyard house model with Mies.

The curriculum at IIT, 1938–75

In the field of architecture today everything seems to be allowed. That is why it is a joy to find an architect who has clearly and consistently adhered to the 'law with which he started' – like Mies van der Rohe. 'Only where our purposes are realized in a meaningful structure can there be talk of architecture.' In 1937 in New York Mies himself wrote down his 'law' in his 'Program for architectural education' as an introduction for the School of Architecture at Armour Institute of Technology in Chicago (later IIT). Committing this law to paper was preceded by months of intensive discussions with his friends from the Bauhaus (Dessau and Berlin), Ludwig Hilberseimer and Walter Peterhans, together with his Bauhaus students John B. Rodgers, William Priestley and Howard Dearstyne, who worked with him from the beginning on the program of the new school in Chicago. The basic theories he wrote down were embodied in the teaching program (Curriculum AIT Bulletin 1939) and established in the 'Principles of Architecture', IIT Bulletins since 1949. These five fundamentals of architecture, viz. structure, space, proportion, material and the fine arts in building, constitute the teaching of the last two years of architectural training and lead the students to the baccalaureate and subsequent professional practice. A special course leads to the 'Master of Science' (now 'Master of Architecture') – to the application of the principles at the highest possible level of design. From the outset a great deal of work is done on the model in order to train and aid the eye. Fine drawings on the drawing board help to develop technical and structural composition. Rhythm and proportion are clarified with collages and fostered by the assurance of hand and eye. The main emphasis is always on the possibilities and limitations of structure, to the exploration of which five years of training are devoted. It is surprising how many variations can still be created out of this basic attitude even today. Mies used to say: 'Architecture has nothing to do with self-expression. All great buildings have said something about an age, not a man.'

Mies' sketch (1960) shows ideas for aluminum sections. Vertical organization of the curtain wall with secondary mullions. Mies said: 'I-beams of drawn aluminum give greater freedom and a more shaft-like appearance than those of rolled steel.'

William Priestley:
Mies' program for architectural education

The program (p. 26–27) was developed by Mies van der Rohe and submitted by him in 1937 to Armour Institute at the request of John Holabird, architect, James Cunningham, chairman of the Board of Trustees, and Henry Heald, president of Armour Institute.

The program was approved as submitted and in September 1938 Mies came to Chicago to be director of the Department of Architecture of Armour Institute, and to be architect of the proposed new campus. Armour Institute subsequently became part of Illinois Institute of Technology.

The program was developed in the New York office of Rodgers and Priestley, who assisted Mies with the drawing of his first commission in the USA. In developing the program he was assisted by them and by Howard Dearstyne, all of whom had been students of Mies when he was director of the Bauhaus in Germany.

Walter Peterhans of the Bauhaus faculty gave great assistance, and developed in detail the parts of the program dealing with visual training, graphics, aesthetic theory, and history of art and architecture.

Mies also drew upon the experience of Ludwig Hilberseimer, who came to Chicago and developed the program in city planning, and of Lilly Reich in all aspects of the design of interiors. All of them had been faculty members of the Bauhaus and the two latter associated with Mies in professional practice.

All of the above were, at various times, members of the faculty at IIT except Lilly Reich, whom personal responsibilities prevented from coming to the USA.

The original delineation of the program was made by William T. Priestley under the direction of Mies van der Rohe. The original was lost. This presentation, following the original layout, was made by Frank F. Ake, Jr., an IIT architecture student, in 1973, under Mr. Priestley's direction.

It is important to note that architectural education at IIT has been able to be very flexible in responding to the new developments which have occurred since 1937 while still following the general principles of Mies' 'Program for architectural education', which are as valid today as they were then.

25

Program for architectural education

Means

Form

Creation of elementary building forms
Based on, and including detailing of, types of construction in:

Wood, stone, brick, steel, concrete

Various combinations of the above materials

	Construction	Material
Wood	Different methods of wood construction	Where and how obtained / how worked / Physical properties / Structural properties / Aesthetic qualities
Stone	Different methods of stone construction	Where and how obtained / how worked / Physical properties / Structural properties / Aesthetic qualities
Brick	Different methods of brick construction	Where and how made / how worked / Physical properties / Structural properties / Aesthetic qualities
Steel	Different methods of steel construction	Where and how made / how worked / Physical properties / Structural properties / Aesthetic qualities
Concrete	Different methods of concrete construction	Where and how made / how worked / Physical properties / Structural properties / Aesthetic qualities
Filling, surfacing, enveloping and other materials	Application of these materials in various types of construction	Where and how made / how worked / Physical properties / Structural properties / Aesthetic qualities

Purposes

Interior furnishing

materials
construction
purpose
arrangement

Analysis of various functions of buildings

Dwellings	Single-family dwelling / Multi-family dwelling / Apartment house / Hotel / Club / Resort / Dormitory / Institution
Commercial building	Store / Office / Display space / Bank / Restaurant / Warehouse
Industrial building	Light manufacturing / Heavy industry / Assembly plant
Public buildings	School / Library / Church / Auditorium / Theater / Museum

Professional training

Architectural drawing

Freehand drawing   and

Structural design

Specifications	Estimating	Financing	Law

Mathematics   and

The nature of man

The nature of human soc

General theory

...s and ...nied communities

According to
the social requirements of:
dwelling
work
public administration
recreation
culture

and according to
the technical requirements of:
topography
kind of building development
hygiene and sanitation
transportation

Reorganization of existing cities
regional planning

Planning and creating

Dependence upon the epoch:
the material structure
the functional structure
the spiritual structure

an analysis of the supporting and
compelling forces of the times

Possible principles of order:

the mechanical — as overemphasis of the material
and functional

the idealistic — as overemphasis of the ideal

the organic — as the determining factor for
the essential significance and
proper proportioning of the purposes
and functions of the various parts
and their relation to the whole

The elements of architectural form:
wall and opening
surface and depth
space and solid
material and color
light and shadow
lightness and massiveness

The structure of architectural form:
The dependence of architectonic structure upon
distinct forms of organization and working methods

The obligation to realize the potentialities
of organic architecture

Architecture, painting and sculpture
as a creative unity

Architectural drawing	
Life drawing	
Structural design	
Mechanical equipment and design	
...ervision	Office practice
natural science	

Analysis of technics
Analysis of culture
Culture as obligatory task

Inaugural address as Director of the Department
of Architecture at Armour Institute of Technology,
Chicago, November 20, 1938 (translation)

All education must begin with the practical side of
life.
Real education, however, must transcend this to
mould the personality.
The first aim should be to equip the student with
the knowledge and skill for practical life.
The second aim should be to develop his personality and to enable him to make the right use of this
knowledge and skill.
Thus true education is concerned not only with
practical goals but also with values.
By our practical aims we are bound to the specific
structure of our epoch. Our values, on the other
hand, are rooted in the spiritual nature of men.
Our practical aims measure only our material progress. The values we profess reveal the level of our
culture.
Different as practical aims and values are, they are
nevertheless closely connected.
For to what else should our values be related if not
to our aims in life?
Human existence is predicated on the two spheres
together. Our aims assure us of our material life,
our values make possible our spiritual life.
If this is true of all human activity where even the
slightest question of value is involved, how especially is it true of the sphere of architecture.
In its simplest form architecture is rooted in entirely functional considerations, but it can reach up
through all degrees of value to the highest sphere
of spiritual existence, into the realm of pure art.
In organizing an architectural education system we
must recognize this situation if we are to succeed in
our efforts. We must fit the system to this reality.
Any teaching of architecture must explain these
relations and interrelations.
We must make clear, step by step, what things are
possible, necessary and significant.
If teaching has any purpose, it is to implant true insight and responsibility.
Education must lead us from irresponsible opinion
to true responsible judgment.
It must lead us from chance and arbitrariness to
rational clarity and intellectual order.
Therefore let us guide our students over the road of
discipline from materials, through function, to
creative work. Let us lead them into the healthy
world of primitive building methods, where there
was meaning in every stroke of an axe, expression
in every bite of a chisel.
Where can we find greater structural clarity than in
the wooden buildings of old? Where else can we
find such unity of material, construction and form?
Here the wisdom of whole generations is stored.
What feeling for material and what power of expression there is in these buildings!
What warmth and beauty they have! They seem to
be echoes of old songs.
And buildings of stone as well: what natural feel-
28

ing they express!
What a clear understanding of the material! How
surely it is joined!
What sense they had of where stone could and
could not be used!
Where do we find such wealth of structure? Where
more natural and healthy beauty?
How easily they laid beamed ceilings on those old
stone walls and with what sensitive feeling they cut
doorways through them!
What better examples could there be for young architects? Where else could they learn such simple
and true crafts than from these unknown masters?
We can also learn from brick.
How sensible is this small handy shape, so useful
for every purpose! What logic in its bonding, pattern and texture!
What richness in the simplest wall surface! But
what discipline this material imposes!
Thus each material has its specific characteristics
which we must understand if we want to use it.
This is no less true of steel and concrete. We must
remember that everything depends on how we use
a material, not on the material itself.
Also new materials are not necessarily superior.
Each material is only what we make it.
We must be as familiar with the functions of our
buildings as with our materials. We must analyze
them and clarify them. We must learn, for example, what distinguishes a building to live in from
other kinds of building.
We must learn what a building can be, what it
should be, and also what it must not be.
We shall examine one by one every function of a
building and use it as a basis for form.
Just as we acquaint ourselves with materials and
just as we must understand functions, we must
become familiar with the psychological and spiritual factors of our day.
No cultural activity is possible otherwise; for we
are dependent on the spirit of our time.
Therefore we must understand the motives and
forces of our time and analyze their structure from
three points of view: the material, the functional
and the spiritual.
We must make clear in what respects our epoch
differs from others and in what respects it is similar.
At this point the problem of technology of construction arises.
We shall be concerned with genuine problems –
problems related to the value and purpose of our
technology.
We shall show that technology not only promises
greatness and power, but also involves dangers;
that good and evil apply to it as to all human ac-
tions; that it is our task to make the right decision.
Every decision leads to a special kind of order.
Therefore we must make clear what principles of
order are possible and clarify them.
Let us recognize that the mechanistic principle of
order overemphasizes the materialistic and func-
tionalistic factors in life, since it fails to satisfy our

feeling that means must be subsidiary to ends and our desire for dignity and value.

The idealistic principle of order, however, with its overemphasis on the ideal and the formal, satisfies neither our interest in simple reality nor our practical sense.

So we shall emphasize the organic principle of order as a means of achieving the successful relationship of the parts to each other and to the whole. And here we shall take our stand.

The long path from material through function to creative work has only a single goal: to create order out of the desperate confusion of our time.

We must have order, allocating to each thing its proper place and giving to each thing its due according to its nature.

We would do this so perfectly that the world of our creations will blossom from within.

We want no more; we can do no more.

Nothing can express the aim and meaning of our work better than the profound words of St. Augustine: 'Beauty is the splendor of Truth.'

The architectural curriculum
(AIT Bulletin 1939–40)

The curriculum of the Architectural Department is designed not only to equip the student with the knowledge and ability required for the professional practice of architecture but also to give him a cultural education to enable him to make the right use of this knowledge and ability.

Architecture in its simplest forms is concerned primarily with the useful. But it extends from the almost purely practical until in its highest forms it attains its fullest significance as pure art. This relationship leads to a curriculum which makes clear, step by step, what is possible in construction, what is necessary for use, and what is significant as art.

This is accomplished in the curriculum by so interrelating the different fields of instruction that the student is always conscious of, and is always working in, the whole sphere of architecture in its fullest sense of designing a structure for a purpose, ordering it so that it attains significance as art, and working out the conception so that it may be realized in the executed building.

At first, the courses are concentrated on training the student to draw, not only to master this technical means of expression, but also to train his eye and hand. Then courses are introduced designed to give the student a feeling for the expression of and relationship between form, proportion, structure, and materials, and to clarify his ideas concerning them. Next, the student will study the materials and construction of simple wood, stone, and brick buildings and then the structural possibilities of steel and concrete. This work is studied in such a way that the significant relationship between the materials, the construction, and the architectural expression is made apparent.

The knowledge of materials and construction leads to a study of function. The functions of the principal kinds of buildings are studied on the basis of an exact analysis. This analysis establishes wherein each architectural problem is distinguished from every other; wherein the real essence of each problem lies. After the essentials of each problem have been clearly established, buildings are designed whose conception and expression are based on these essentials.

The study of function is carried beyond individual buildings into groups of buildings and then into communities in the field of city planning in order to demonstrate the interdependence of all building in relation to the city as an organic whole.

The curriculum leads naturally from the study of the means with which one builds and the purposes for which one builds into the sphere of architecture as an art. This is the synthesis of the entire curriculum; the fundamentals of the art of architecture; the artistic principles, the means, and their expression in the executed building. The student applies the principles in free creative architectural design and works his design through in collaboration with the construction staff of the department.

31

In conjunction with the curriculum there is a clarification of the cultural situation today so that the student may learn to recognize the sustaining and compelling forces of his times, and to comprehend the intellectual and spiritual environment in which he lives. The material, intellectual and cultural aspects of our era are explored to see wherein they are similar to those of former epochs and wherein they differ from them. The buildings of the past are studied so that the student will acquire from their significance and greatness a sense for genuine architectural values, and because their dependence upon a specific historical situation must awaken in him an understanding for the necessity of his own architectural achievement.

For the fuller accomplishment of these objects a year of study in addition to the regular four-year program is recommended so that the student may have the opportunity to integrate his basic education.

Chicago possesses an architectural tradition from which have come the most significant American architects. Through their work they have decisively influenced the development of contemporary architecture. The Art Institute with its rich collection of ancient and modern art, its permanent exhibit of applied art, and its temporary art exhibits; the Field Museum with its natural history, prehistoric and ethnological collections; the D.H. Burnham Memorial Library, one of the most significant purely architectural libraries in the country; and the Ryerson Art Library help to create an artistic atmosphere in Chicago especially favorable to the study of architecture.

Architecture: Synopsis of the 5-year curriculum
(IIT Bulletin 1944–45)

The Institute offers advanced work in Architecture
leading to a degree of Master of Science in Architecture. Students graduating with the degree of
Bachelor of Architecture from an accepted college
are eligible to enroll in the course leading to the
master's degree in Architecture. The degree is
awarded upon completion of the work in Architecture 501 and 502 and upon the preparation and acceptance of a thesis. The work in Architecture 501
and 502 depends upon performance, not time, and
culminates in the thesis. Graduate students will be
permitted to undertake the thesis when they have
developed and demonstrated their ability to do independent creative architectural work of high
standing. Graduates of other architectural departments or schools will normally require at least one
year of study before the thesis.
Graduate study serves to clarify, to intensify, and
to provide the opportunity of delving profoundly
into the problems of the Art of Architecture.
Architecture is rooted with its simplest forms entirely in the useful, but it extends over all the
degrees of value into the highest sphere of spiritual
existence, into the sphere of the significant; the
realm of pure art. Therefore, the study of architecture is concerned not only with its material side,
materials, construction, and purpose, but also essentially with its fundamentals as an art. An understanding, discussion, and clarification of the cultural questions of our epoch are also necessary.
Furthermore, it is important to study the buildings
of the past in order to obtain from their greatness
and significance a sense for genuine architectural
values. Their dependence upon a specific historical
situation should awaken an understanding for the
necessity of our own architectural accomplishment.
The object of the advanced work in Architecture is
the clarification of:
The structure as an architectural factor; its possibilities and limitations.
Space as an architectural problem.
Proportion as a means of architectural expression.
The expression value of materials.
Painting and sculpture in their relationship to architecture.
The application of these principles by means of
free creative work.
During this course all work will be solved on the
basis of fundamental principles, whereas the work
on the thesis will be based on a given situation and
will be carried out independently.

Mies van der Rohe:
Peterhans' Visual Training Course at the
Architectural Department of IIT
(Chicago, February 5, 1965)

When friends and students of Walter Peterhans
decided to publish a selection of plates from the
Visual Training Course he developed at Illinois Institute of Technology, I was asked to write an introduction to the publication because of the part I had
played at the inception of the course.
In 1930 when I took over the Bauhaus in Dessau,
Walter Peterhans was head of the Department of
Photography. There I became acquainted with his
painstaking work with the students, and the great
discipline he taught and demanded of them. Not
only was he a photographer second to none, but a
strong personality with a broad education in many
fields, notably in mathematics, history and philosophy.
When I came later to Chicago to head the Department of Architecture at Illinois Institute of Technology, I asked Ludwig Hilberseimer, a leading
theoretician in city planning, and Walter Peterhans
to become members of the faculty and to work
closely with me in initiating our own curriculum
for training and educating young architects.
Confronted with the problem of changing a school
containing students at different levels, from freshmen to graduates, it was obvious that the only possible starting point was at the freshman level. As
properly trained freshmen progressed from level to
level, a curriculum conforming to our ideas and
conconant with our aims could gradually be
evolved.
It was my conviction that any freshman, given the
right exercises and guidance, could become a good
draftsman in one year. I asked Peterhans to set up
a course to this end, so that at the upper level we
would have students to our liking. He succeeded
admirably, and in the course he organized a foundation was laid for clean, clear, exact work – the
basic prerequisite for what was to follow.
Somewhat later I made the startling discovery that
although the students appeared to understand what
I said about the importance of proportion, they did
not demonstrate the slightest sense for it in their
exercises. I realized that their eyes simply could not
see proportion. This problem was discussed with
Peterhans and we decided to introduce a new
course, especially designed for training the eyes
and forming and maturing a sensitivity for proportion. It was to be a continuation of the basic freshman course, but starting at the sophomore level. To
achieve this end, Peterhans developed the course
he called Visual Training. The effect of the Visual
Training Course was a radical change in the whole
mental attitude of the students. All fussiness and
sloppiness disappeared from their work; they
learned to discard any line that did not fulfill a purpose, and a real understanding of proportion
emerged. Although specially gifted students some-
times produced plates that would have enriched
34

the collection of a museum, the purpose of the
course was never to produce works of art, but to
train the eyes.

Walter Peterhans: Visual Training

'Visual Training' is a course which serves to train
the eye and sense of design and to foster aesthetic
appreciation in the world of proportions, forms,
colors, textures and spaces.
It comprises exercises which are on the one hand
sufficiently abstract to show visual qualities in isolation from one another – in crystallized form as it
were – disentangled from the complexities in which
they occur in architecture, in industrial forms and
in the fine arts, and yet at the same time concrete
enough to allow these and variations to be tied to
specific technical media and prescribed conditions.
And finally copious and flexible enough to exist entirely in their own right in that they are pure repre-
sentations of visual qualities and relationships, intensified to the maximum, aspiring to maturity and
fullness, so that they are, as of their own accord,
consummated in free harmony and ultimately allow technical media and conditions to be forgotten.
By nature visual training is one of the bases for the
specialized work of the architect and the industrial
and graphic designer. It is no substitute for their
work but stimulates, permeates and controls it in
exercises which can be repeated from time to time
when the need for them is felt. They put things in
perspective and allow them to be approached again
at a deeper level. The course affords access to the
common sources from which the formal values of
the fine arts and architecture take their rise, and
likewise the ideas and concepts which are indispensable for the analysis and criticism of a work of
art.
We attach incomparably more importance to visual
training than freehand drawing or drawing from
the nude. Sketching is indispensable as a means of
recording an idea, clarifying it and communicating
it to others; but as a means of fostering insight and
stimulating ideas visual training has quickly shown
itself to be a greatly superior method since it begins
at a deeper level in training the eye for architec-
35

tural conception and quality and for formal creation in the widest sense. (It has therefore had an important influence on perspective, representation, and model building in the architectural department and has in turn embodied valuable suggestions made in that quarter.)

We have studiously avoided arbitrariness in the name of personal freedom of expression. We do not mould clay with our elbows, nor do we entertain any illusions about the significance of giant wheels made of folded paper. We make experiments but we deliberately refrain from making all possible experiments. Even in practical physics experiments are directed, otherwise we should never have progressed beyond the Magdeburg hemispheres and patterns of iron filings in a magnetic field. Nevertheless we have made radical changes in traditional methods and at the same time we have subjected them to a permanent check on their utility. We endeavor to isolate aesthetic qualities from one another and to display them in an intensified form. We then combine them in a 'quite different' whole in which they are transcended – say, in a space which is generated out of themselves. This calls for the strictest mental discipline and critical acumen – characteristics which are much rarer in students than the desire to indulge in free experimentation, and which must therefore be all the more deliberately fostered. This combination of a sense of quality with mental discipline and critical acumen is what we are really anxious to cultivate in the student and what determines our working method.

37–83

Undergraduate study.
36

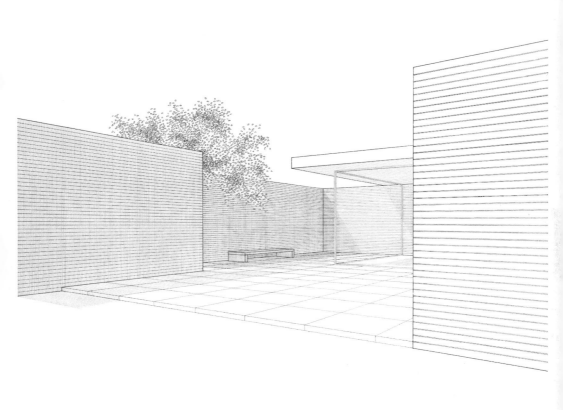

All 'Visual Training' studies are on Strathmore cardboard upright format 20 × 30″ and some of the other student studies on oblong format 40 × 30″.

Perspective and drawing exercise. Mies van der Rohe's house at the Berlin Building Exhibition 1931 is taken as a basis (1st year).

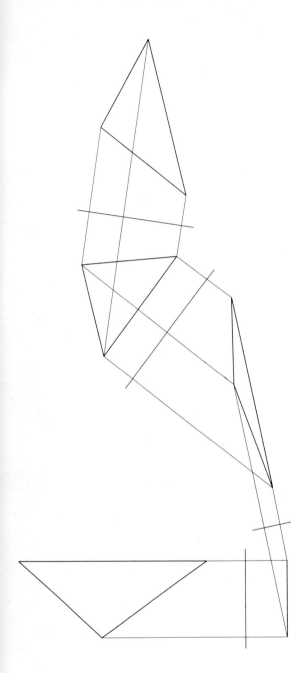

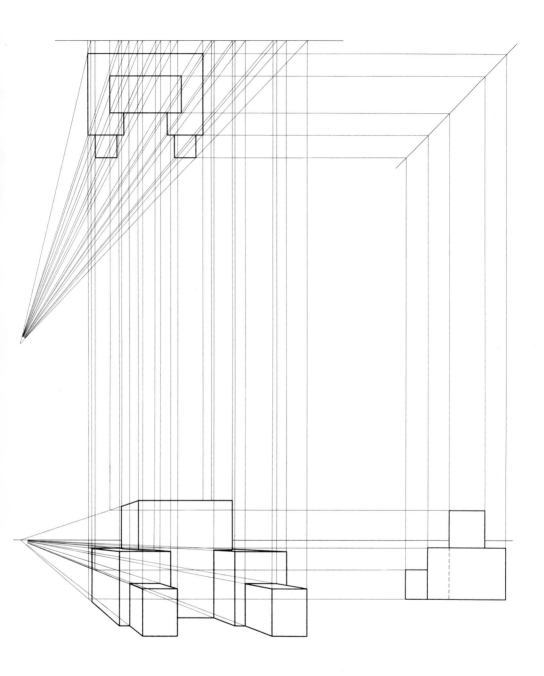

Perspective drawing and descriptive geometry.
Development of the student's imaginative ability,
his powers of observation, and his sense of spatial
relationship by descriptive geometry (38) and perspective projection (39) in the study of these basic
principles (1st year).

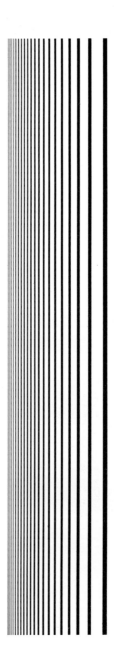

40–45

Visual training.
Aesthetic expression as experience. Exercises in the study of form, proportion and rhythm, texture and color, mass and space. Exercises in visual perception and aesthetic judgment. Isolation and analysis: interdependence and integration of sensuous qualities. Aesthetic unity under restrictive conditions.

40

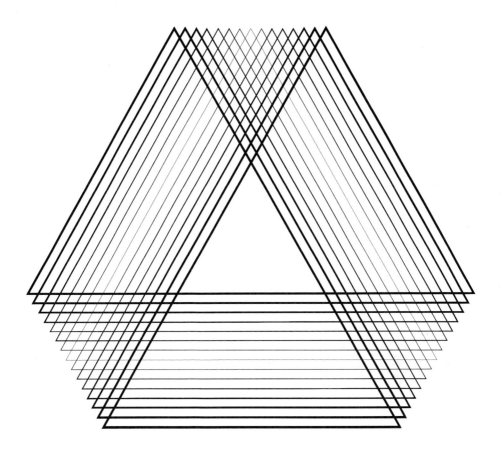

Line drawing exercise. The parallel arrangement of
the most simple rectangular plane surfaces of equal
length is a stipulation. Width, sequence and distance apart are to be determined in such a way that
black and white clarify each other and cohere in a
whole (1st year).

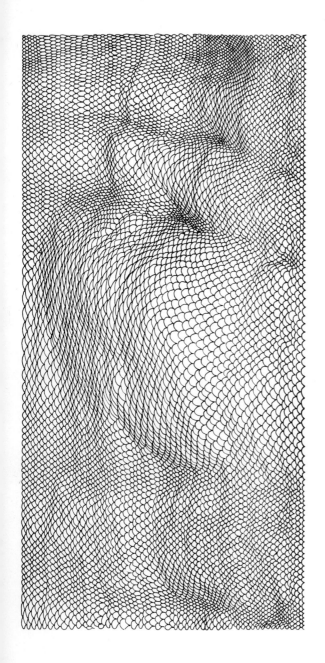

Variations of texture. Rhythms and modulations.

Texture exercise. Collage of textured materials.
Texture, color, quantity and reciprocal position
are balanced with meticulous precision. Inter-
mediate spaces and boundary lines were treated
as essential elements of the composition (2nd year).

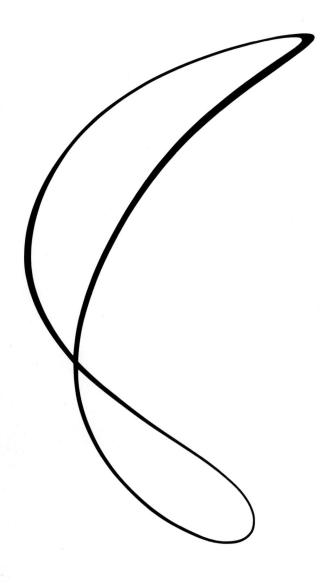

Exercise with curves. Curves conceived not as an
independent ornament but enclosing a space and
imbedding it in, and combining it with, the surrounding space.

Parabola example. Elements of the composition
are the networks of straight lines, resulting in
curves and gray tones whose intensity depends on
the density of the straight-line systems.

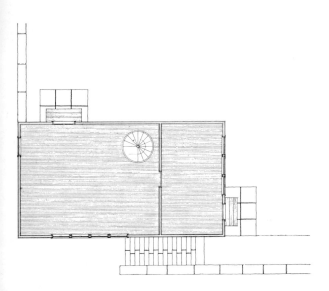

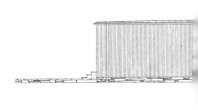

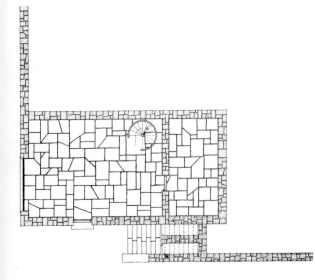

46–63

Materials and construction.
Analysis of the natural building materials: wood,
stone and brick; construction on the basis of their
properties. Elemental wood, stone and brick buildings, their methods of construction and their architectural expression. Transmission of this knowledge in the form of architectural and construction
drawings.

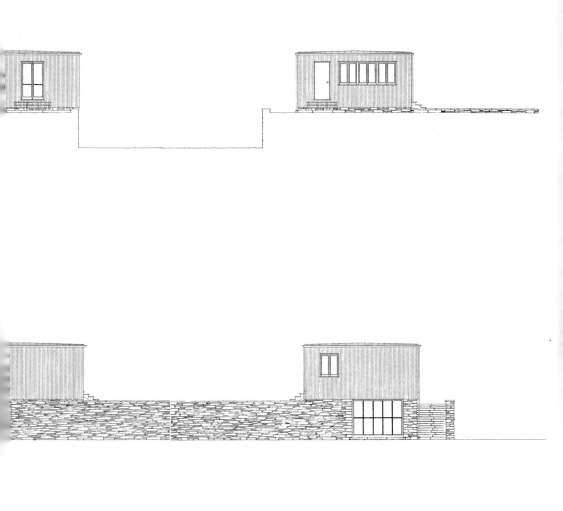

46–49

Development of a house constructed in wood with basement of stone, 1940 (2nd year).

Plan of the basement and ground floor. Front elevations of the wood house.

47

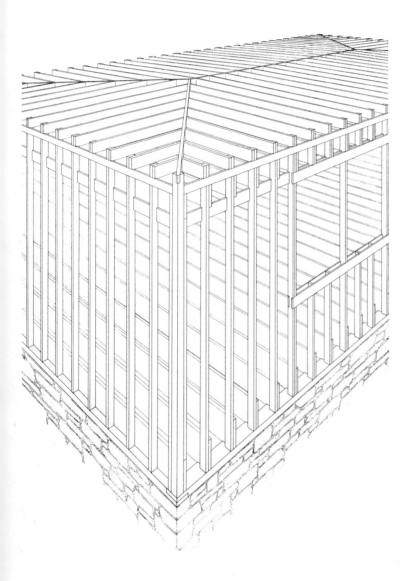

Structural detail of balloon-frame construction.

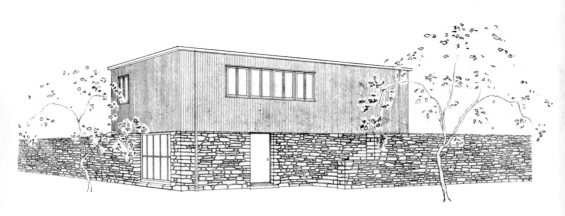

Perspective drawing, wood and stone construction.

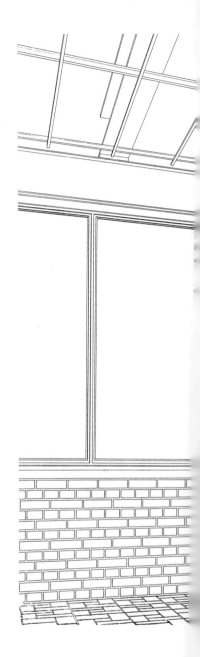

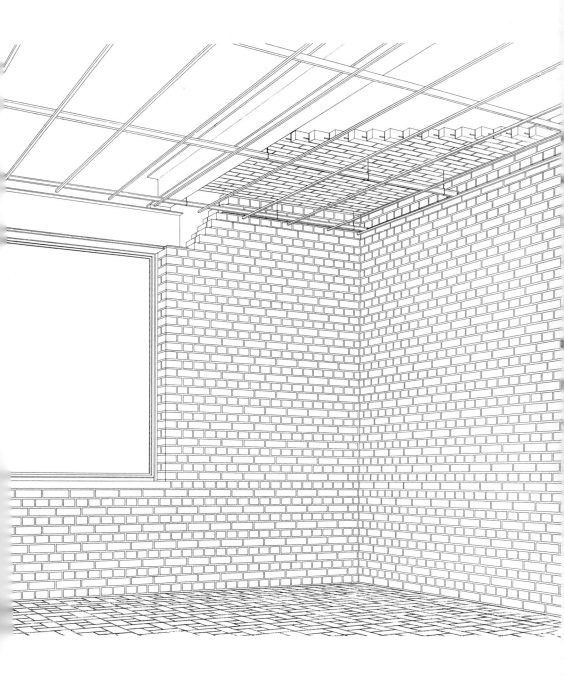

Corner detail showing floor, wall and ceiling of
brick building.
51

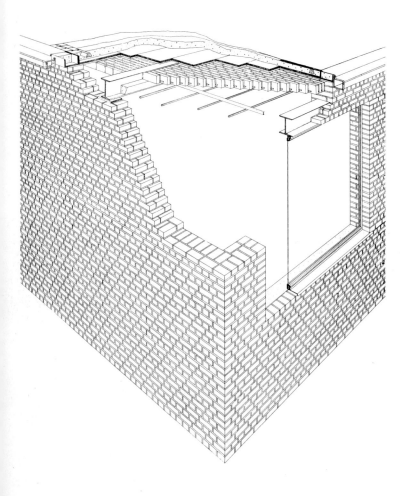

Wall construction in cross-bonding.

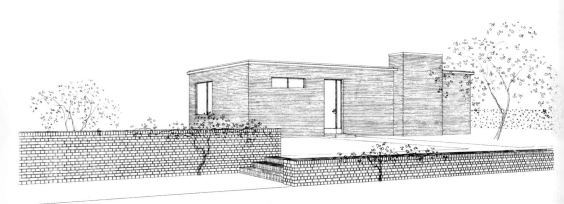

Trees and planting sketched by Mies 1940.

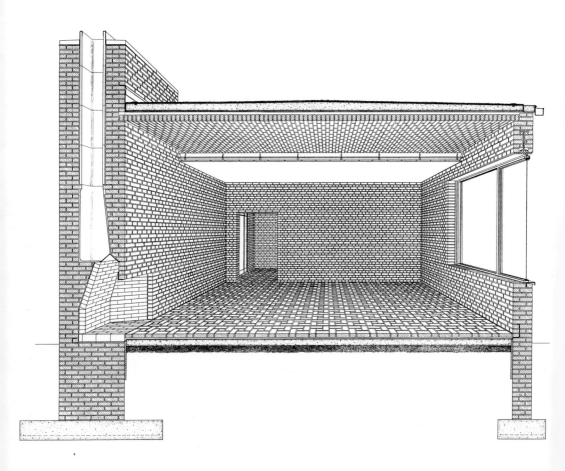

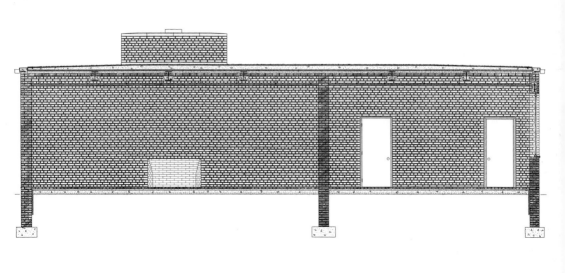

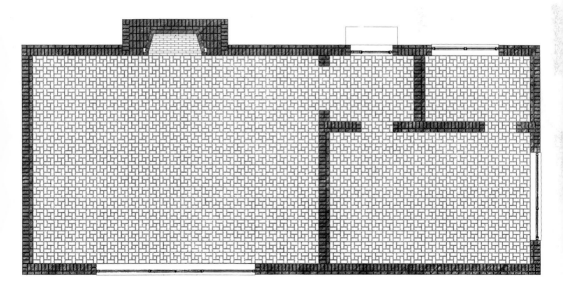

Perspective section (54) plan and section (55) of
brick house showing fireplace (2nd year).
55

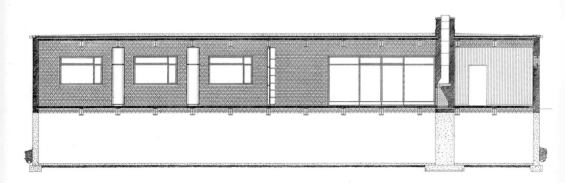

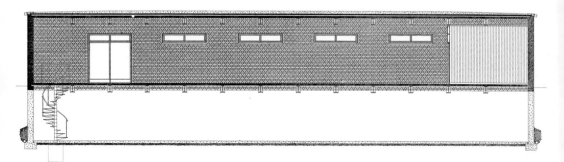

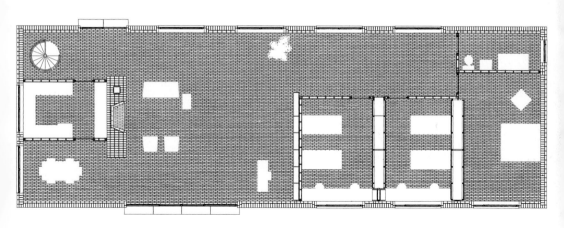

56–59

Dwelling house of exposed brickwork with three bedrooms (3rd year).
57

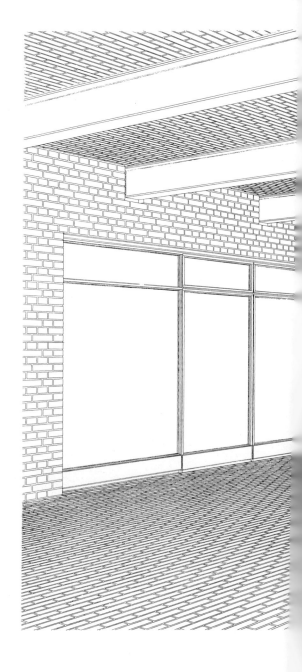

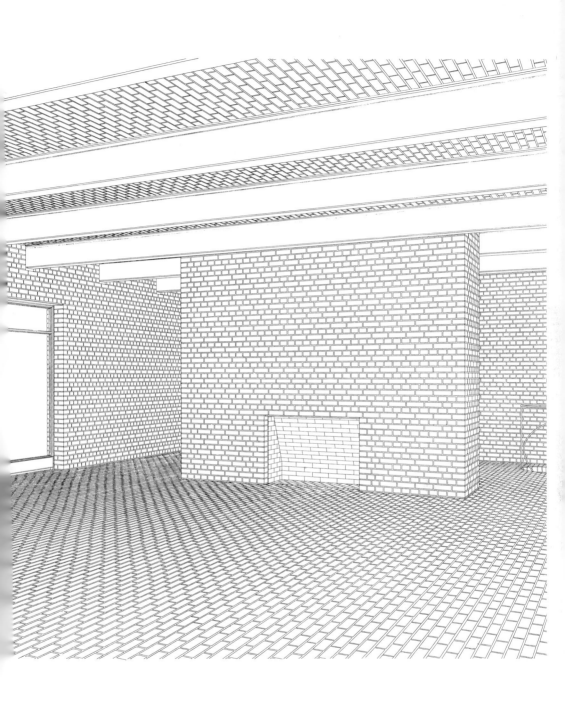

Free-standing brick wall with fireplace. Exposed
steel beams with flat roof slab of reinforced brick.

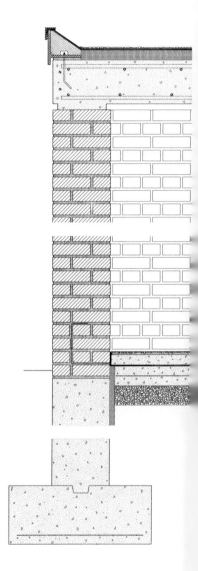

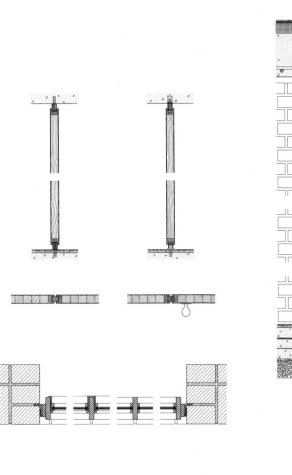

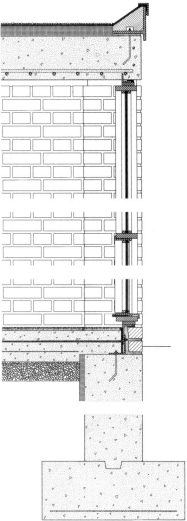

Vertical and horizontal section showing load-bearing brick wall and reinforced concrete flat roof slab.

Two-story row houses with load-bearing party
walls of exposed brickwork (maisonette type)
(3rd year).

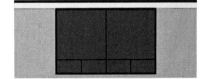

64–73

Space and proportion.

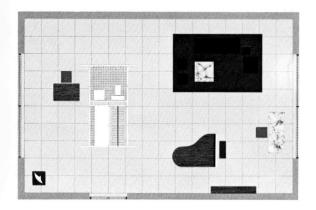

64–67

Collage studies of a simple dwelling house with
load-bearing brick walls (4th year).

Collage study: Music room as architectural
problem and its relationship to sculpture.
67

Exercise in space and proportion, using model,
scale ¼″ = 1′0″.

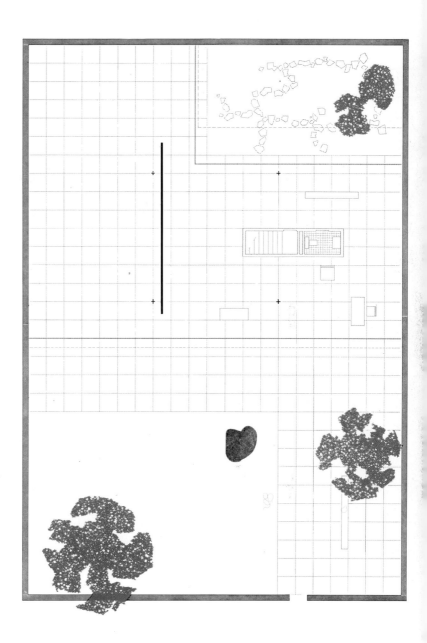

69–71

Collage study of a house with two courts
(4th year) with exterior brick walls.

69

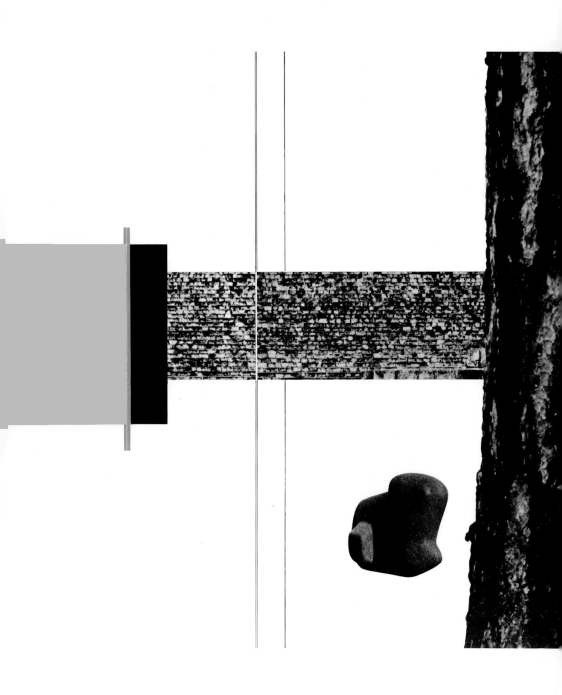

Collage showing external court wall and interior
partition wall with steel column.

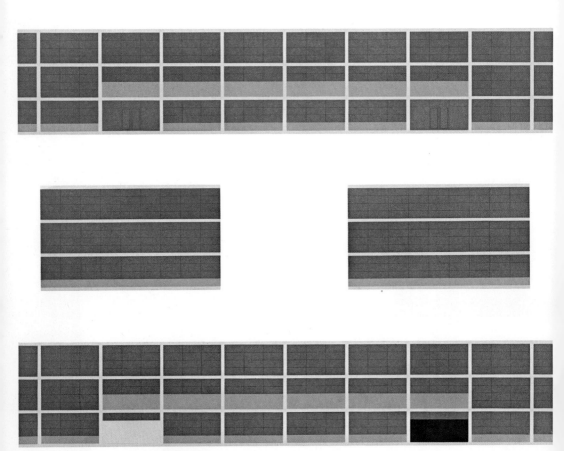

72–73

Collage elevation. Expression of the skeleton construction in concrete and steel.

Concrete skeleton with cantilevers (5th year).

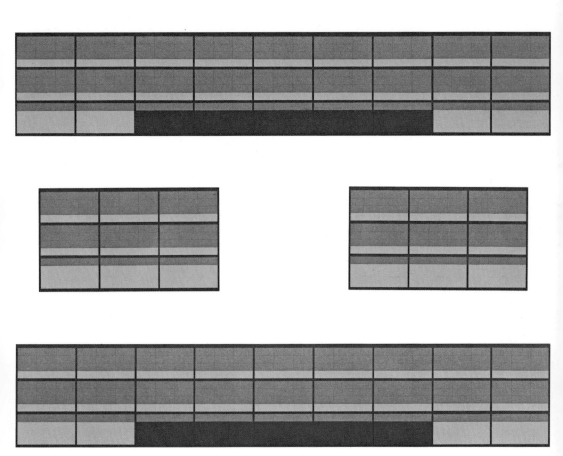

Steel skeleton (5th year).

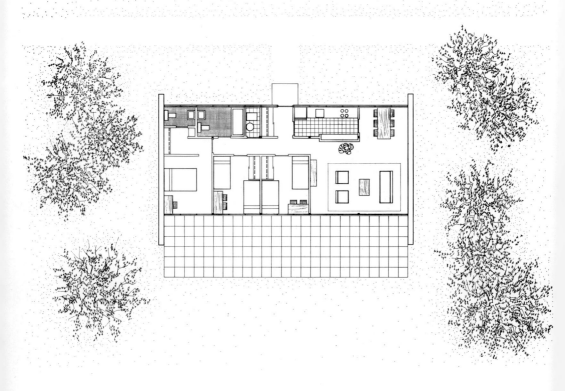

74-79

Dwellings and housing. The theory of dwellings.
The influence of orientation, social hygiene, living
requirements, and population density on the development plans. The relationship of the house to the
lot, to the neighboring lots, and to the street. The
different types of dwelling and kinds of building
development, and their relationship to each other.

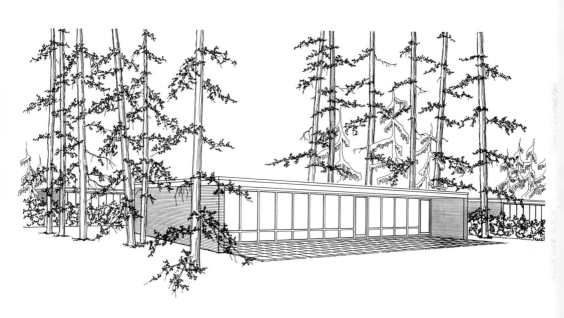

74–75

Single-family dwelling (950 sq.ft.).
Perspective study of houses in the environment.

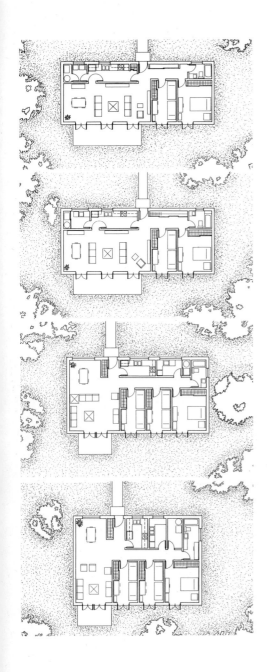

Housing, varying floor plans.

Housing, structural system.

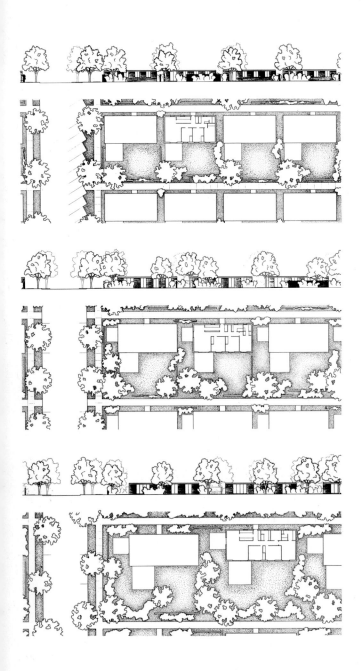

Housing, size variations.

Single-family housing, L-houses.

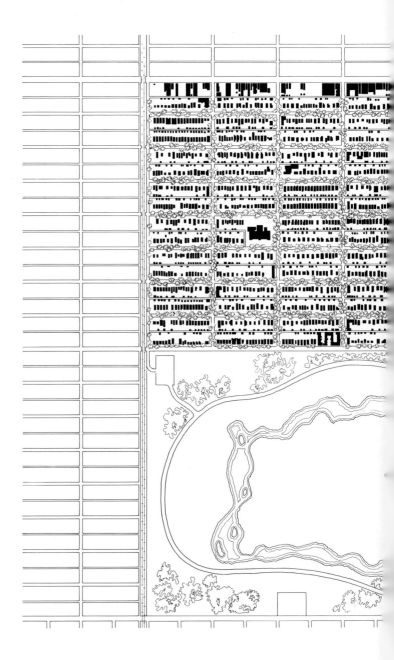

80–83

Student work under the direction of Rimantas Pencyla.
Marquette Park redevelopment plan in Chicago.
Application of planning principles to the redevelopment of a specific site.

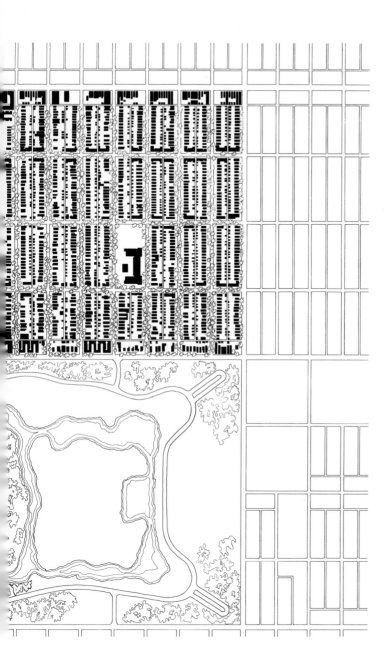

Existing building (density 8.9 D. U. acre).
81

Proposed plan (5th phase) (density 8.5 D.U. acre).
82

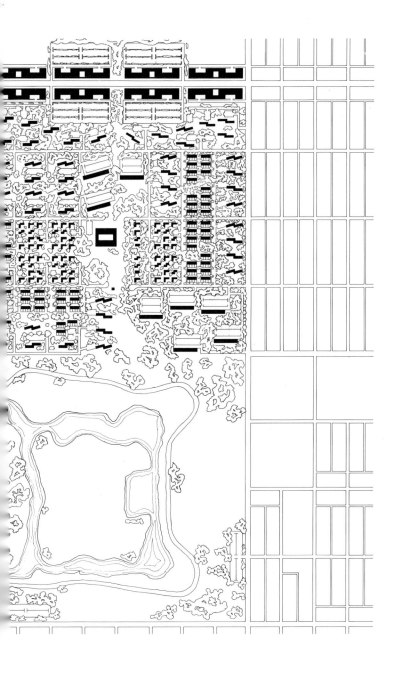

Theses submitted for the Degree of Master of
Science in Architecture
in the Graduate School of IIT

Many problems of structural architecture which
Mies set himself in his work were first discussed
with his students and then examined from all an-
gles with the aid of sketches, collages, models and
plans. It often happened that one of his students
then took over this problem and made it the subject of a scientific and architectural study which he
submitted as a thesis. The result was a model with
the most precise details of material and construction, space and proportion. To the outsider these
studies may appear to be very dependent on Mies
but they are variations with a character of their
own, although within a definite objective framework, and it is immaterial whether the master or
the student created them. In the first two theses
presented here we have examples of problems set
by Mies himself. The majority of the theses were
written after Mies had left the staff in 1957 and
tackle new questions of current interest but invariably they still display the high standard of the school
of Mies in their results.
From the outset the principles formulated in these
theses were extended to the large-scale building going on in the center of Chicago. In the skyscraper
types of building we find proposals and solutions
which were later taken over and implemented by
the big offices of Chicago. During the last ten years
the frame-tube load-bearing system has been
developed in Chicago for high-rise buildings.
Dr. Fazlur Khan, an engineer of the school of
Mies, said: 'This constructional system was selected
to show that it is quite possible to replace present
urban planning with its high building density and a
number of medium-high buildings by a few very
high structures of this kind. In this way large open
spaces would be gained at pedestrian level as well
as a much more inviting and interesting environment.' The way the school of Mies has continued to
develop the wide-span framework and weave
variations round the Miesian conception is exemplary. There is a thesis on prefabricated dwelling
houses. This line of advance represents another
step for the school of Mies: to the standard of quality are now added the problems of quantity. As an
institution the school of Mies does not stand still. A
new opportunity was afforded to develop ideas
when at IIT the Departments of Architecture, Planning and Design were amalgamated (1975) under
the new direction of James Ingo Freed (also one of
Mies' students). This might prove of great importance if the school of Mies succeeds in incorporat-
ing design (Dietmar Winkler, new chairman of the
Institute of Design since 1976) into its terse and precise formulation of necessary structure and technical 'know how', as Mies himself succeeded in
doing with his furniture for the Barcelona Pavilion.

Thesis by Myron Goldsmith, 1953:
'The Tall Building: the Effects of Scale'
86-story high-rise building

General considerations
Unlike Europe, America did not feel under any obligation to an architectural heritage and could
therefore develop the principles of modern architecture unimpeded. The booming city of Chicago
during the last third of the 19th century provided
the local architects with an opportunity to realize
vast skyscraper projects of steel and glass. Skeleton
architecture took shape in Chicago on an entirely
new and permanent basis.
Logical detailing extracted the ultimate from steel
and glass. In this connection I recall a dictum of the
sculptor Constantin Brançusi: 'Simplicity is not the
end, but perfection.' An equally terse aphorism –
'less is more' – erroneously attributed to Mies was
actually coined by Peter Behrens. It originated
when his students and associates were on vacation
and showed him their freehand sketches.
The name Myron Goldsmith occurs most frequently in connection with the school of Mies. He is
today one of the most distinguished of Mies'
pupils. Between 1945 and 1950 he worked in Mies'
office on the Farnsworth House and was the first
student to develop a bold engineering and architectural project for a skyscraper as a graduate study at
IIT under Mies. With his thesis 'The Tall Building:
the Effects of Scale' Goldsmith initiated in the early
fifties the examination of structural problems in
high-rise buildings. The work concluded with this
result: 'Every structural type, whether an organism
or an artifact, has a maximum and a minimum size.
In the tall building there are two limitations on
height: one is structural and the other is functional.
When a certain magnitude has been reached in a
tall building, the structural system must be
changed. A new structural system gives the possi-
bility of a new architectural expression.'

Technical development
Goldsmith's 86-story high-rise project consisted of
a primary structure of reinforced concrete – a main
load-bearing structure of 8 haunched columns
with floor slabs at intervals of 15 stories – which
was to be erected first. Secondary structures of
various types could then be inserted into the inter-
mediate spaces thus created.

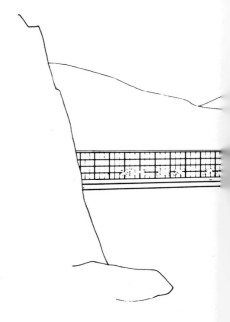

84–95

Graduate study.

85–89

Thesis (Master of Science in Architecture of the
Graduate School of ITT)
submitted by Myron Goldsmith:
The Tall Building: the Effects of Scale, 1953.

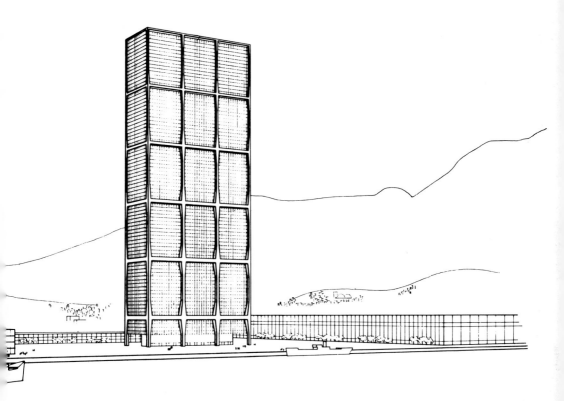

Proposal for an 86-floor high-rise building with a
primary reinforced concrete structure.

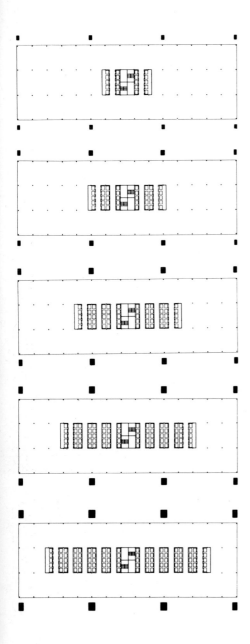

Typical plans for the five main floors.

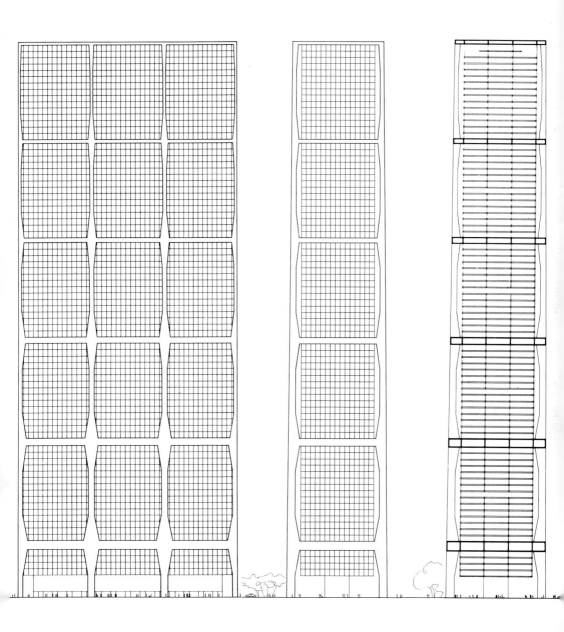

The main load-bearing structure of 8 haunched columns with floor slabs at intervals of 15 floors is first erected. The secondary rooms can then be inserted in the spaces.

Thesis by Conrad Roland, 1959:
'An Arts Center', a space-frame construction

General considerations
The principles of systematic construction of the
school of Mies are dominant in building theory
and design. The columns and the roof slab determine the appearance of the building. There can be
no question of wanting to overrate the idea of
structural design. If we think, however, of the architectural chaos up and down the country where
every house must look different from its neighbors, or where monotonous rows and blocks stand
side by side, the idea of structual architecture, if
adopted, would certainly lead to greater harmony
in the general scene. Our rural settlements with
their uniform half-timbered buildings in which
each facade nevertheless displays great variety are
living witnesses of such a harmony and devoid of
all schematism. In the present babel of formal language and social pretension adherence to structural
design might open new avenues for us and above
all restore the optical balance.

Spatial organization
Conrad Roland came from Berlin in 1958 in order
to continue his studies at IIT. He was one of the
last students to have his work corrected by Mies.
The aim of the thesis 'An Arts Center' was to clarify
the spatial conditions that must be fulfilled in order
to accommodate a collection of modern sculptures
in a large exhibition hall in a way that is meaningful. A square hall with sides of 240×240 feet was
placed on a terrace.

Technical development
The 'Mero' frame system comprising tubes and
'Mero' joints was used for the roof and the walls.
The tubes are screwed into the joints. The girder
grids are formed by joining up square-based pyra-
mids. The large roof slab rests upon four grid
structure columns of triangular shape arranged at
the outer edge and is cantilevered far out to the
corners. On his return to Berlin in 1962 Roland
once again revised this project together with Frei
Otto in a kind of filigree and lightweight construction.

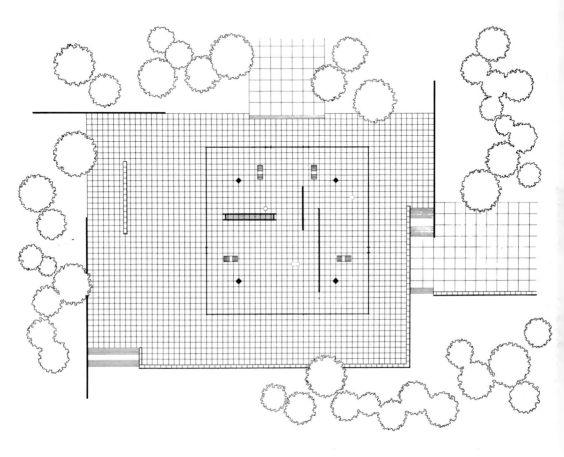

90–95

Thesis submitted by Conrad Roland:
An Arts Center 1959.

Building and open space on the great terrace.

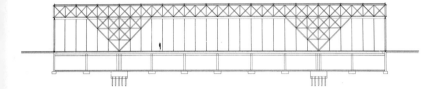

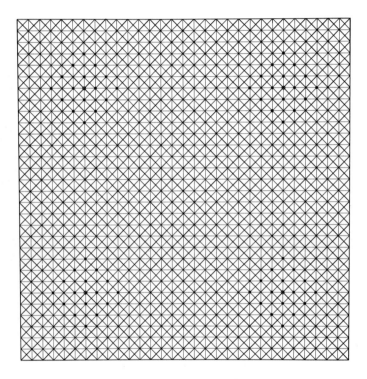

Section and plan of the grid structure with four interior lattice columns.

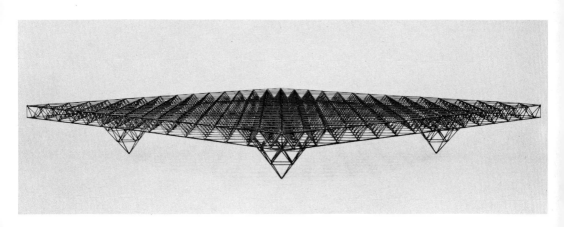

The possibilities and limitations of construction are
tried out on the model.

The load-bearing structure of the hall is a spatial
framework to be enclosed above and at the sides
with Mero standard elements – a prefabricated
steel construction system.

95

Aphorisms by Mies 1955

Architecture once depended on the directed skill
of the craftsman. It was oriented to his slow,
meticulous ways, bound by his primitive technology
and guided by a firm system of values. When
the Machine Age brought new materials and new
tools, new forms emerged.

Possibilities of the new technology gave the
architect a sudden freedom from age-old
limitations and objectives. He could vacillate
between capricious self-expression and subser-
vience to economic demands. More permanent
values tended to lose definition. In a civilization
where the premium was on cheapness, speed,
utility and superficial stage effects, there was no
room for the craftsman.

Parallel with the "irrelevant slip-cover civilization"—as Walter Gropius called it—another
civilization was growing up. Powerful dams,
monumental grain elevators, beautiful highway
interchanges, elegant transmission towers, lacy
suspension bridges grew out of the earth and
immeasurably expanded man's vision of form.
They carried within themselves new objectives,
new limitations and new laws.
Forms are developed toward high aesthetic
refinement by artist-engineers. "Whenever
technology reaches its real fulfillment, it
transcends into architecture."

Architects appear who use the new technical
potentials and with them reach for basic form.
Their new discipline is self-imposed. Their
asceticism is the thirst to partake in the primary
source of Being. They show that abstract elements
of contrast, rhythm, balance, proportion and
scale become real only when distilled through the
character of materials; they live only when they
express methods proper to those materials
and harmonize with the forces that act in them.
It is the craftsman who determines the quality
of these existential forms and he thus finds his
way back to architecture.

Yet the achievements of pure technology still
challenge architects to meet the spiritual needs of
men in an equally convincing way. For
"architecture depends on facts, but its real field
of activity lies in the realm of significance."

George E. Danforth:
Architecture and planning at the Illinois Institute of Technology, 1959-75

'Architecture is rooted with its simplest forms entirely in the useful, but extends through all the degrees of value into the realm of pure art.'
This basic statement made by Mies van der Rohe some thirty years ago is the foundation upon which he and his colleagues, the late Dr. Ludwig K. Hilberseimer and the late Professor Walter Peterhans developed the curriculum of the Department of Architecture and Planning at what is now the Illinois Institute of Technology in Chicago, Illinois. It is upon that philosophical framework that the work in the school has continued to be developed since Dr. Mies van der Rohe's retirement as director of the Department of Architecture in 1957.
The curriculum concentrates on fundamentals in the hope that the student may gain a clear grasp of principles. Work in each subject proceeds from the simple to the more complex. The place of each subject in the curriculum as a whole has been carefully and logically determined so that each study will enlarge upon the experience and understanding derived by the student from preceding exercises.
In the development of the undergraduate curriculum from the first through the fifth and final year the student first learns his crafts, and when he has mastered the craft of architecture and planning he is prepared to study its arts. Coincident with the basic craft indoctrination is the development of the student's reasoning powers and his senses. As an architect, he must have an understanding of construction to work logically and imaginatively with engineers, but as an architect he must also learn to construct with his eye, so to speak. Thus, the refinement of visual perception begins with his first practical exercises in drawing – both architectural and freehand drawing. The student must learn to draw with clarity, precision and facility.
Drawing to the architect is what writing is to a writer. It is his prime means of communication. While the student is learning to draw expertly, he is simultaneously learning to respect perfection generally. We believe that the first-year student who learns to distinguish between a fine and coarse pencil line will have an instinctive feeling for the thickness of a window mullion when he becomes an advanced student. While studying simple construction in wood and brick during the second year, and steel and concrete in the third, he is gradually learning that not only wood and brick, but all materials have special properties which must be understood in order to use them in an architecturally correct manner.
A great deal of emphasis is placed upon construction, for it is our objective, inculcated in the students from the beginning of their studies, to achieve a structural architecture, an architecture growing out of structure, but elevating structure to the level at which it transcends mere engineering,

98

and invites evaluation on an aesthetic basis. Mies has said, 'great buildings are characterized by their clear construction, and their architecture is in the proportions.' Therefore, a method of work, which should be the essence of architectural education, must make clear that construction and an understanding of structure are the soundest bases for developing a genuine architecture, removed from the realm of individual whim to the realm of understanding and insight.

Exercises in visual training provide the student with the opportunity of making aesthetic expression a part of his experience. His eyes are trained to recognize significant relationships of form, proportion and rhythm, texture and color, mass and space.

The study of function in buildings is the foundation of all advanced work in architecture and planning. Here the elements of planning are given concentrated attention. Again, as in the entire curriculum, study projects are always of the greatest simplicity. At no phase of his development should the student be confused or misled by work made complicated arbitrarily. At this point we are not interested in the solution of specific problems, for in these there always resides the danger of working for specific rather than basic answers. Our prime concern is to direct the training towards general principles. Hence the work begins by considering the rooms of a house, such as kitchen, bathroom and bedroom, in which the plans are determined by the needs and uses of the equipment and furniture contained within them, due attention being paid to which orientation of the sun is possible, tolerable, desirable.

After investigating the individual elements of a house, the total complex is studied, proceeding from a simple, single house, to simple groups of houses, apartments, schools and other building types, again taking into account function, orientation and density. Utilizing a specific housing unit, possibilities and consequences of different densities are examined. Functionalism is not a goal in itself. It is rather a means to the attainment of the goal of a rational architecture. It is assumed, without question, that a building must function well, but this would not justify it as architecture. The student must learn how to interpret function just as he does construction, but he must interpret these essentials in terms of ultimate architectural expression.

It is significant in the curriculum that during the third year of study the advanced courses in architectural construction are concurrent with the aforementioned courses in function. These two main courses in the third year are very closely related in that the particular projects in function are frequently the same problems given in the construction work.

At the completion of the third year the student, equipped with his craft, structural, visual and planning experience, is ready to consider the more elusive and theoretical aspects of architecture. Our entire curriculum, after all, is aimed at these.

99

The architecture and planning courses in the fourth and fifth years are in essence a synthesis of the knowledge and skills acquired in the first three years and together they form an entity. As in the previous courses the problems are concerned first with simple architectural elements in which the student examines the refinements of space, materials and proportion. In what we call the bearing-wall problem, the arrangement of the space within and the penetration of the outside walls by windows and doors are carefully studied.

A subsequent problem goes beyond the bearing-wall structure and introduces the student to the problems of open spaces or free planning. Each student constructs a model in which he first places one wall in the given space and then by gradually increasing the number of walls he experiences the reciprocal reaction of these several elements and the given space. Through this abstract exercise and its development into an open-plan house the student should begin to grasp the complex and intangible interrelationship of spaces. After this stage the problems advance to large buildings of more varied purpose.

Skeleton construction, whether it be steel or reinforced concrete, is the structural system most widely employed in our time for buildings of size. Very special architectural problems are posed by this structural principle and for this reason the student, by means of scale models, investigates the architectural possibilities of both low and high skeleton buildings. Different enclosing elements are studied; various solutions are developed and, as with all exercises, the student makes an exhaustive comparison of the various possibilities.

When the student has gained an understanding of the problems of single buildings he proceeds to a study of the relationship between buildings, and amongst groups of buildings. Involved in such projects, which constitute the synthesis of the curriculum, are buildings of greater complexity – museums, libraries, auditoria, churches. At every stage and level the study is directed towards an uncovering of general principles.

Today the architect deals not only with single buildings as in the past, but with entire areas of the city. Therefore, in the fourth year the student is concerned with principles of planning, developing certain elements of planning, their relationship to each other and, finally applying these principles to the replanning of cities. In such a sequence of work the student gets to understand the real meaning of urban renewal which is not an end in itself, but rather a means of gradually changing the city. For architectural students intending to enter the planning profession a planning option is offered in the fifth year.

In a program of education the objective of which is to establish order, method and clarity in every phase of the work a rigorous discipline is imposed upon both students and faculty. Such a discipline reflects an acceptance of the objectivity which is characteristic of this technological age and which the student must understand to enable him to function intelligently in his future practical work.

City and regional planning
(IIT Bulletin 1968–69)

Throughout history man's relationship with his environment has continually been changing as he modifies it with new technical developments. This implies that the interaction between man and his environment can be creative or destructive.
The aim of planning is to bring about a harmonious relationship between man, technics and nature. It is the means by which a human environment can be developed.
The aim of the department is to seek broad principles involving fundamental relationships from which to develop solutions to planning problems. We neither seek nor apply rules and formulas. Since the task of the planner is to help create a human environment, he must develop the ability – from the basis of fundamental knowledge – to understand the human situation broadly, to analyze, to discover what is important and to synthesize work from many diverse and special fields into a whole, leading not only to solutions of difficult problems but also to the expression of social aims and aspirations.

Theory of city planning.
Residential areas. The block system and its historical development. Traffic and residential areas. The
street system with the residential area and its dif-
ferentiation. Park areas and playgrounds and their
connection with residential areas. Business areas
and their traffic and parking problems. Redevelopment of different parts of the present-day city.

Business quarter (Chicago South Side) with residential area on both sides of the traffic development (Prof. Hilberseimer's regional planning course).

103

Undergraduate studies

The elementary exercises in the curriculum of IIT as Mies and his team established it have remained basically unchanged down to the present day. To the outsider this education and its tendencies seem monotonous and sterile. Accurate drawing and optimal consideration of detail do, however, create a sound basis for the building process. Perfection and precision should always take first place in practice (not only in the school of Mies). The point of these exercises is to train the perceptive powers to grasp the interrelationships and integrations arising in specific current problems. Theoretical training in the principles of architecture is fostered in city-planning exercises. However, in this study we shall not pursue the subject of the manifold exercises in city and regional planning at IIT; since Ludwig Hilberseimer's death in 1967 this department has been conducted by Paul Thomas. Hilberseimer's ideas on city planning must await publication in a more competent quarter. The IIT curriculum serves to solve architectural problems in terms of fundamental principles. It is not the What? but the Why? that underlies its demands. The student's task is to recognize the structural nature of architectural problems and to solve them in creative freedom. According to Mies, real works of architecture are very rare and they are almost invariably technological structures.

Analyses of historical and modern buildings,
1973–76, R. Ogden Hannaford's course

It is not a simple task to adapt the catalogue of
what has to be learned as regards education,
knowledge and skill to new needs and yet still
retain the basic conception of the five principles of
architecture. One of Mies' collaborators over many
years, the architect Ogden Hannaford, who is now
a professor at IIT, conducts a course on art history
with the focus on the analysis of buildings. The
American student, who is, of course, not very
familiar with the European scene in art history, is
made to draw buildings of historical architectural
importance during his first semester. Great importance is attached to the quality of the draftsman-
ship and to the style of presentation on uniform
'Strathmore' drawing papers. In this way the
student acquires spatial imagination and is confronted with the process of construction.
Mies repeatedly called attention to the relationships between structural features within a stylistic
period. By making drawings the student learns by a
process of analysis what these criteria are and at
the same time acquires skill as a draftsman. One of
Mies' educational principles was: 'Great buildings
of the past are studied for their essential significance and their original architectural value. Their
origination from a specific historical situation
should throw light on the necessity of original architectural creation.'

Ogden Hannaford:
Architectural History –
an experiment in mass education

If the study of architectural history needs any justi-
fication, it may be sufficient to recall that a single
lifetime is never long enough to observe at first
hand the vast array of extant buildings and wind-
swept ruins that tell of man's experiments in arranging the built environment. Historians have
loaded our libraries with surveys and monographs
to record those adventures, but a student in architecture with only a few hours a week left for history
cannot hope in one semester to examine more than
a few of those volumes. A hundred students,
however, not duplicating the task but dividing the task,
could multiply their education a hundredfold if
they could effectively exchange the results of their
individual efforts.
An introductory course, designed to provide that
opportunity, is offered to 120 freshmen in their first
semester. Illustrated lectures present material from
times and places related to the particular theme or
category selected for individual studies in that year.
In weekly discussion groups of twenty students the
project is outlined and each student gets a specific
building to investigate and to draw. The first job is
to find the source material in the school's library,
or wherever it may be obtained. Plans and sections
are all drawn at the same scale (1:240) to make the
relative sizes of the buildings apparent when they
are displayed side by side. Site plans and towns,
when possible, are held to the ratio of 1:2500. The
format is uniform to bring out important differ-
ences of character and construction among the examples compared. The medium is ink on illustra-
tion board, with titles large enough to be legible
when a photo slide of the drawing is projected on
the lecture screen. A brief historical statement
together with an annotated bibliography is written
by the student to accompany the graphic presentation.
An exhibition of all the drawings is mounted a
week before the end of the semester. In an hour's
walk through the gallery the students can 'read the
term paper' of every classmate. It may also occur to
them that a slide of their drawing might be used to
illustrate a point in some lecture to a future class.
Architecture is its own language and, next to the
building itself, a fine drawing is the least ambig-
uous and most nearly instantaneous medium of
communication among architects. It shows views
the camera cannot capture and reveals qualities no
text can convey.

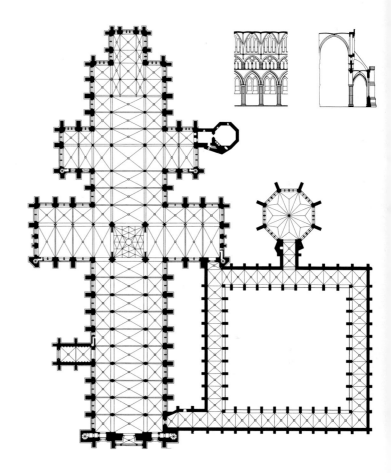

105–111

History of architecture. Undergraduate study.
Ogden Hannaford's course 1973–76.
A historical survey of architecture, showing structure and expression as development of the spiritual, social and technological status of cultures.

Cathedral Church of St. Mary, Salisbury (England),
1220–75 (scale 1:1250). (Drawing by Peter Blinn)
107

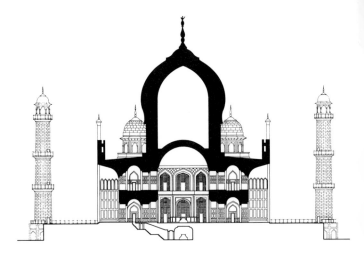

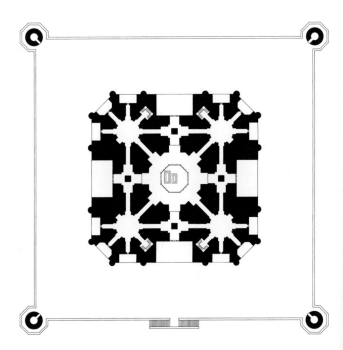

Agra: Tâj Mahal (India), by Makramat Khan,
1632–43 (scale 1:1250).
(Drawing by Timothy J. Anderson)

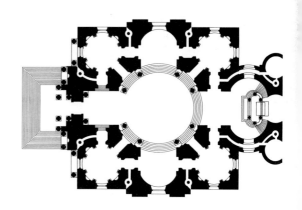

Paris: St-Louis des Invalides (France), by Jules
Hardouin Mansart, 1675–1706 (scale 1:1250).
(Drawing by Sarah K. Lavicka)

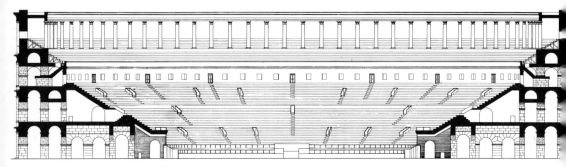

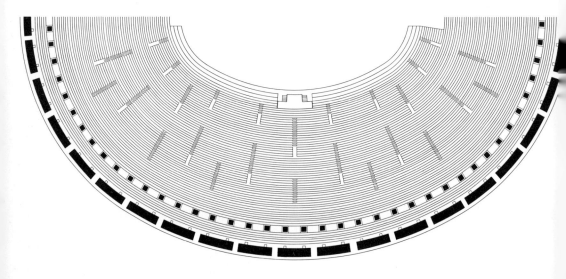

Rome: The Colosseum (Italy), by Vespasian, 70–82
A.D. (scale 1:1250). (Drawing by Peter J. Eckroth)

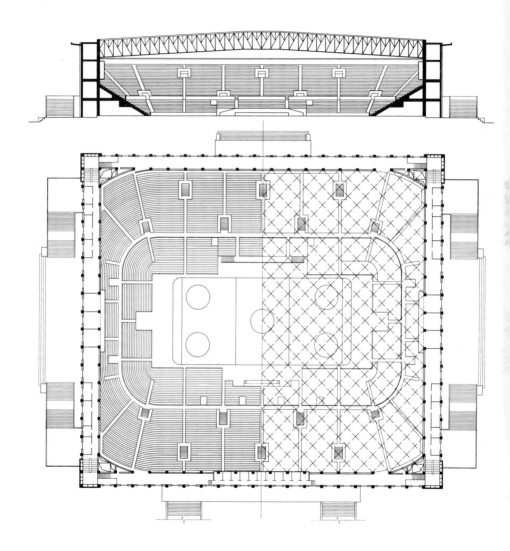

Peking: The Capital Indoor Stadium (China), 1966
(scale 1:1250). (Drawing by Steven Chiu Min Au)
111

Undergraduate study 1973-74 'Loop Renewal',
Daniel Brenner's course

The exemplary cases presented here are not intended to teach a lesson and certainly not to preach the
supremacy of the school of Mies. In the confusion
of modern trends these examples have held their
own for many years and have forfeited nothing of
their basic thinking. All these solutions demand a
conjunction of brain and hand in which thinking
should be consonant with manual work at the
drawing board and in practice. Time and again it is
said that the architecture of Mies is no longer rele-
vant. However, it is not fashion that interests us but
carefully thought out structural design. Architecture cannot be recreated every week. The 'novel' is
an epiphenomenon – only the 'good' can be the
aim.
The institution of the 'Chicago School of Architecture Foundation' is technically competent to play
an important part in preserving what is worthwhile
from the buildings of the pioneer period and to
teach the principles they stand for. In Chicago it
was suggested that the conversion of these office
blocks into dwelling units in order to bring life
back to a dead business district should be set as a
theoretical exercise at IIT. It was therefore easy to
make new proposals for the use of the historic office buildings of the 'Chicago School of Architecture' (Rookery, Reliance and Monadnock Buildings). At the same time the transport problem had
to be reconsidered and no building under a preservation order could be altered during the renovation
work. Here the principles Mies expounded are applied to problems of preservation and reutilization.

Daniel Brenner:
The Loop Renewal Project

Before starting their thesis, graduate students who
have not gotten their Bachelors at IIT spend a preliminary orientation year. Coming as they do from
just about every place in the world but the United
States, this gives them a chance to adjust to a
strange environment and acquire some insight into
our philosophy and the forces shaping a 'developed' industrialized country. A part of this year is
devoted to a Chicago-related problem. The city is a
magnificent laboratory and has a generous share of
the universal urban ills.
This past year we started with a study based on the
proposed new Loop subway. Only two of the nine
graduate students involved came from a country
with a subway; Mexico and France. The others
were from Nigeria, Iran, Korea, India and the Phil-
lipines and while unfamiliar with underground
transport, had a good share of pollution, noise,
deterioration, dirt, traffic and overcrowding in their
native cities.
All possible Loop circulation elements were examined including the shortlived AIA proposal for a
new elevated system. The students decided they
were most interested in developing the new stations
(mainly along the Monroe Street connector) as
nuclei for as many different activities as feasible.
By revising Loop traffic patterns for buses, private
vehicles, trucks and pedestrians, a strong physical
tie could be made with the stations, and adjacent
commercial, recreational and hotel facilities could
also be directly related to the focal spaces.
This concentration on what was essentially a system for getting people in and out of the Loop as
quickly as possible somehow pointed up the fact
that a totally transient population might be one of
the Loop problems.
It is not at all uncommon to find central city living
in European cities. Paris is a prime example but
many others have a round-the-clock life and New
Yorkers have long lived cheek by jowl with their
business districts. The Chicago 21 plan recommended residential not only in the old railroad
yards but along the Chicago River on the very
perimeter of the Loop. In New York again, the
venerable Dakota Apartments on Central Park
West are eagerly sought for their grandly scaled
spaces and sturdy turn of the century detailing
while Richard Meier's lower west side Bell Lab
conversion into artists' apartments has had a fine
success.
These indications spurred our investigation of the
Rookery, Monadnock and Reliance for residential
conversion. If workable it would provide an anti-
dote to the glut of new office space threatening the
landmarks and start a more meaningful residency
than the few odd souls who now sleep in at the
Standard, Union League and University Clubs. It
was decided to make apartments which would ap-
peal to top income prospects. They are frequently
less inhibited than the middle class and those at
113

present most close to the Loop are either very rich or very poor. Sutton Place was infiltrated by high class residents when the meat packers were still going full blast next door. Once the rich set up a beachhead, the middle class can't resist and a pattern is established.

The Rookery plans show solutions using single and double loaded corridors and duplexes, all to a Burnham scale and with a multiplicity of bedrooms. The interior court facilitates apartment planning as does the long, narrow shape of the Monadnock which is a natural for apartments. The Reliance is really quite small and the solutions for it are somewhat more modest though still extremely pleasant. No first floor plans are shown for any of the buildings since the intent was to retain commercial tenancy at street level. All three buildings are within a block or less of parking facilities but who needs a car if he has a nest in the Rookery, or a commissary if he's a couple of blocks from Stop and Shop, or a colored TV if he has windows on State Street?

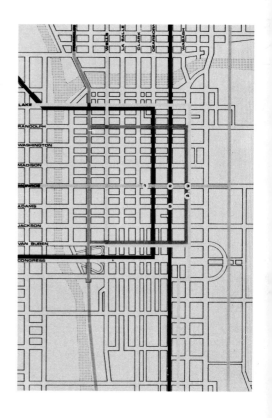

112–121

Renewal in the Loop (graduate study)
Daniel Brenner's course.

Residential: An investigation of the condominium
apartment potential of historic Loop office buildings to foster increased use of the area and insure
maintenance of the landmarks. Transportation:
Studies of major interchange between transportation modes to facilitate movement and interrelate a
maximum of urban activities.

116–117

Rookery Building, 1885–86, Chicago
(Burnham & Root, architects).

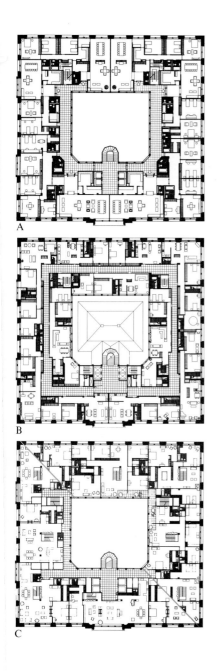

Proposals for apartment plans: (A) Access to
apartments from the interior courtyard corridor.
(B) Apartments giving on to street and interior
court.
(C) Maisonette apartments.

117

118-119

Reliance Building, 1894–95, Chicago
(Charles Atwood, D. H. Burnham & Co., Architect).

Proposals for apartment plans: (A) One 3-room
and one 4-room apartment. (B) One 2-room and
two 3-room apartments. (C) Two 2-room and one
3-room apartment.

120–121

Monadnock Building, 1889–91, Chicago
(John Wellborn Root, Burnham & Root, Architect).

A

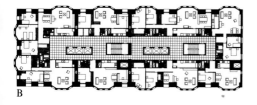

B

C

Proposals for apartment plans: (A) Two 1-, 2-, 3-,
4-room apartments. (B) Four 2-, two 3- and 4-room
apartments. (C) One 3-, 4- and one 5-room
apartment, two 2-room apartments.

121

Undergraduate study 1974
'Chicago Uptown Art Community Center'
David C. Sharpe's course

General considerations
Discussion of the social aspects of architecture with
progressive students at IIT gave rise to a number of
new projects concerned with the clearing and redevelopment of the slum areas of Chicago. The study
'The Douglas Community – A Neighborhood
Development' in the vicinity of IIT, a quarter with
many dwelling houses from the time of Sullivan
and Wright, was divided into three parts: survey,
overall planning, and development of individual
types of building.
A prominent place in this analysis was taken by the
architectural rules (construction, space, proportion,
material and incorporation of works of art – painting and sculpture) which undoubtedly represent
Mies' principles and yet leave scope for the objective character of the construction and for variations.

Technical development
David Sharpe (professor and collaborator of SOM)
has undertaken tasks of this kind. A group of four
students, Alex Bonutti, Miguel Carpio, Paul Chiu
and Ying Lam, planned a Community Art Center
on an existing triangular plot in Chicago by way of
an undergraduate study (5th year). A steel skeleton
with a curtain wall was designed for the three-story
building, in which the columns stand behind the
facade. The drawings show three plan levels with a
section through the building. The collage of the
front elevation shows clearly how subtly the building is planned to blend into the existing situation
and with what mastery the problems of material
and proportion have been solved.

David Sharpe
Community Art Center (5th year project)

The aim of this project is to work with art forms and introduce them to the public not as objects of highest order, but rather as things as close to the daily man as going to work.

The participation of a community is essential to this purpose since it affords every individual the opportunity to practice one or more of the activities called art. The building is thought to become an active volume that responds to simultaneous forms of interaction, no space remaining idle or isolated. It proposes a place where every day people might be able to experience different forms of action which would otherwise be consigned only to 'artists'; to make of art a common thing with the people seems to be a good way to bring back the lost creativeness and enthusiasm of the average person. Private and public expression intermingle with learning and recreation in a space where people can be both actors or spectators, being able to perform and observe as an active group of like beings.

The building will comprise general areas destined for multipurpose uses such as: exhibitions, theater, dance, conference, etc. and also private areas for other types of activities. Also workshops of crafts and graphics, a small library, day care for the children of the people involved, cafeteria, and a limited amount of living space for visiting persons. This seeming agglomeration would be located in a dense urban area in order that its vitality be maintained, and the building would be molded to fit the scale of its surroundings adding to the existing sense.

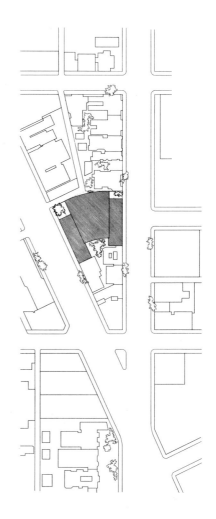

122–129

Uptown Community Art Center in Chicago
(near North Side),
Graduate study. David Sharpe's course, 1973–74.

General plan showing triangular site and existing
streets in Chicago.
124

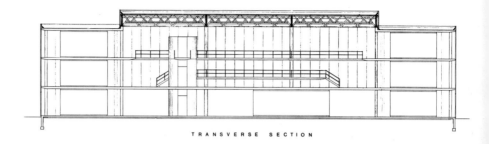

TRANSVERSE SECTION

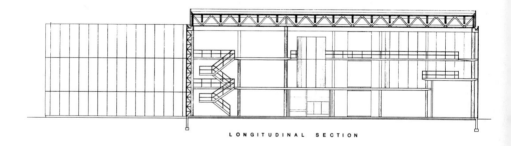

LONGITUDINAL SECTION

The long-span structure provides for flexibility of interior arrangements.

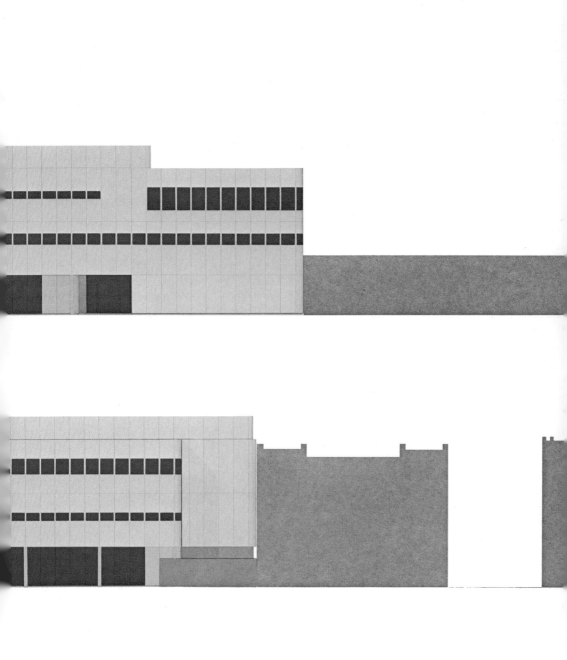

Collage study of elevations with existing buildings.
127

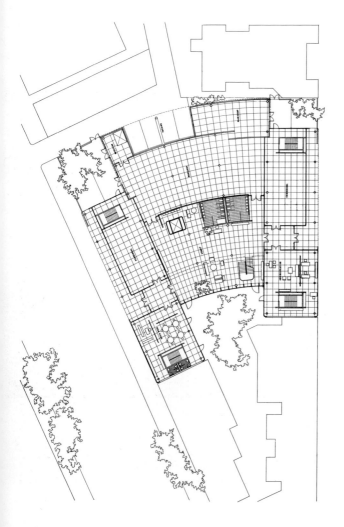
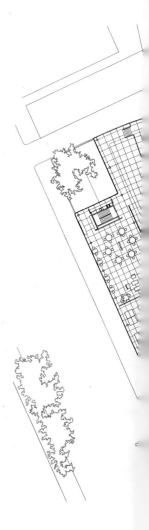

Plan of ground floor (scale ⅟₆₄″ = 1′0″).

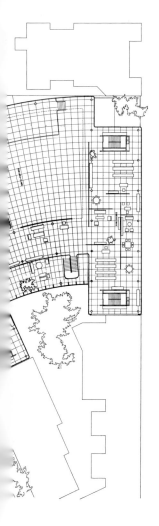
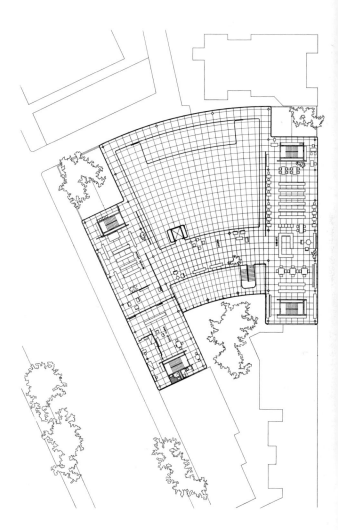

Plan of first and second floors (scale $\frac{1}{64}'' = 1'0''$).

Thesis by Robin Lee Hodgkinson, 1968:
'An Ultra-High-Rise Concrete Office Building'
built on the diagonal system

General considerations
What is involved here is not an attempt simply to
go one higher than the next in Chicago architecture. It is more than a century since the architect
William Le Baron Jenney first constructed a skyscraper as an iron- and later a steel-framed building. The first skyscrapers of the world were built
with a framework of steel and an infill of glass. It
was at that time that the 'Chicago School of Architecture' was formed which, since the forties, has
been continued by the school of Mies. This school,
and particularly graduate studies at IIT, have left
their impress on the present skyline of Chicago.
What appeared in these graduate studies as
something lucid and objective was forced by others
in Chicago to soar ever higher until the world's tal-
lest building was built.
The thesis 'An Ultra-High-Rise Concrete Office
Building' by the Australian student R.C. Hodgkinson under the direction of Myron Goldsmith and
Dr. Fazlur Khan shows as early as 1968 a skyscraper structure consisting of a reinforced concrete
framework with diagonals. Various preliminary
studies resulted in a high-rise project with 116 floors
and a square tower 1427 feet in height and 216
feet along the side. The diagonal pattern of the
frame tubes, which run the height of 24 stories, is
clearly visible.
This new form of bearing structure with diagonals
for very high buildings is replacing the conven-
tional vertical system of column and beam. The
'frame-tube' load-bearing structure, which was
developed in Chicago in recent years, clearly ex-
presses the wall pattern in the design of the facade.

Spatial organization
The Illinois central site in the middle of the 'Loop'
is scheduled as a possible site for this giant skyscraper, in which some 25,000 office staff can be accommodated. The standard module of the offices is
4.6 or 6 feet based on a story height of 12 feet or
room height of 9 feet.

130–133

Thesis submitted by Robin Hodgkinson:
An Ultra-High-Rise Concrete Office Building, 1968.

Location of the study on the Illinois Central Railroad site in Chicago. Besides the three tower office blocks, each 1427 feet high, four Y-shaped 100-floor apartment towers 800 feet high are also included in the plan.

131

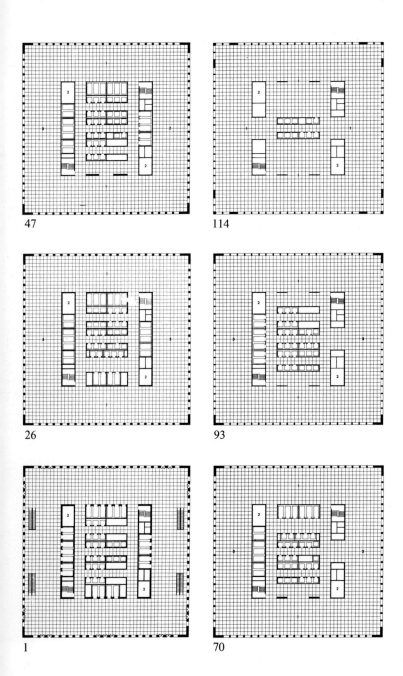

Typical plans: entrance hall (1), 26th, 47th, 70th,
93rd, 114th floors.

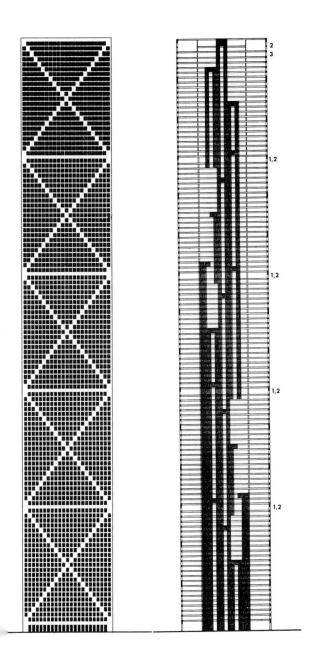

Front elevation and section with 116 floors.

Thesis by Peter C. Pran, 1969:
'An Exhibition Hall with a Suspended Roof
Structure.'

General considerations
Once again we are concerned with buildings with
wide spans. Iron-frame constructions go back to
the early days of the machine age when factory
framed buildings, exhibition pavilions, stations,
market halls and greenhouses took shape. These
were works by the new type of engineer architect.
Today especially we can see in this industrial architecture the finest examples of a clearly thought out
structure. A successful design of this kind was proposed by the architects James W. Hammond and
Peter Roesch in 1969 in a preliminary study of a
grid frame building for the Northbrook Library in
Chicago. It now seems that it will be difficult to im-
plement major projects of this kind during the next
few years because of the worldwide shortage of
money. Nevertheless sports and congress halls with
wide spans are on the drawing boards at Murphy
Associates under the direction of former IIT
student Helmut Jahn.
Peter Pran said: 'Architecturally this hanging truss
construction produces a new aesthetics of size and
lightness of structure. This aesthetic is underlined
by the glazed roof, the glazed walls and the
brilliance with which the natural light penetrates
the space.'

Technical development
The graduate study 'An Exhibition Hall with a Suspended Roof Structure' by Peter Pran under the
direction of the architects Myron Goldsmith and
David C. Sharpe and the engineer Dr. Fazlur Khan
solves the problem of spanning a column-free hall
construction of 1000×2000 feet and the window
wall 100 feet in height by economical means. The
trusses span the shorter dimension. The columns
stand at 164-foot centers and the intervals between
them are divided into 12 fields. An imposing suspended roof structure, comparable in some ways to
the suspension bridge constructions of the 19th
century, spans a hall which is glazed on all sides,
the glass walls extending from floor to ceiling. The
scale of the building is shown by comparing the interior with the models of the DC-8.

134–139

Thesis submitted by Peter Pran:
An Exhibition Hall with Suspended Roof Structure, 1969.

The columns are 241 feet high, each column having
a cross section of 8 × 6 feet.

135

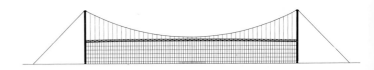

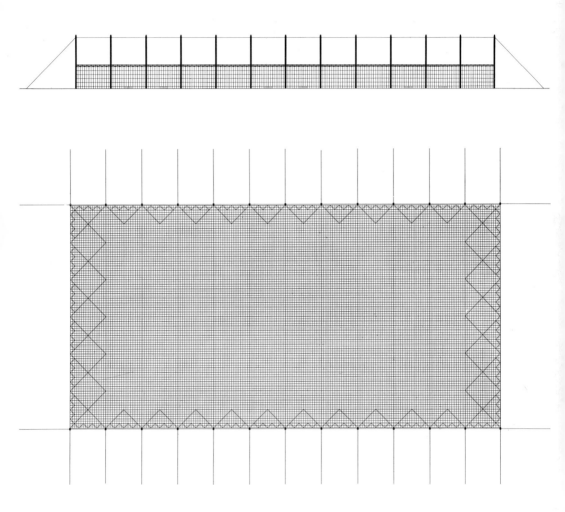

The exhibition hall (universal space) is completely
flexible.

Construction study with cables. The roof is covered
with plexiglass domes.

Thesis by Dennis Peter Korchek, 1969–72:
'A Prefabricated Sheet-Metal House'

General considerations
This important graduate study deals with a prefabricated one- and two-story house of steel elements
combined in two units. In Korchek's thesis priority
of attention is given to the programmatic deploy-
ment of function and production process. The collage and drawing of the inner room with a fully-
glazed facade and the Picasso sculpture and Miró is
intended to show that architecture and works of art
can also be integrated in the dwelling house. The
fabrication process and the design intent are unified in this project. On the one hand we have the
factory product developed in conformity with economic methods of production, and on the other the
living room designed with individuality and imagination.
The design of the prefabricated McCormick house
by Mies van der Rohe 1951–52 was determined by
the facade elements of the tower apartment blocks
on Lake Michigan. The thesis by Korchek 'A Prefabricated Sheet-Metal House', under the direction
of the architect Arthur Takeuchi, contains prefabri-
cation studies for one- and two-story dwelling units
of steel stressed skin modules.

Technical development
Dennis Korchek explains: 'The system of construction devised for this prefabricated house serves as
both the structural system and the enclosing envelope. As a consequence, the number of parts necessary to construct the house has been reduced to 47.
This use of fewer elements is best illustrated in the
typical mullion section, and in the typical floor and
roof sections. Both of these details reflect the
concept of the stressed skin, whereby the interior
and exterior steel shells combine with the honey-
comb and urethane core to form both the enclosing
envelope and the supporting structure, not in the
form of connecting panels but in the form of tubu-
lar modules.'

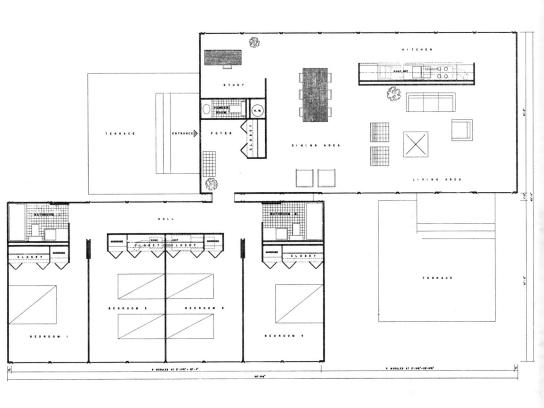

140-147

Thesis submitted by Dennis Korchek:
A Prefabricated Sheet-Metal House, 1972.

Plan of the prefabricated metal house (1850 sq.ft.).

141

This dwelling unit can be shipped by truck in
8 modules which can be joined and erected in the
field in one working day.
143

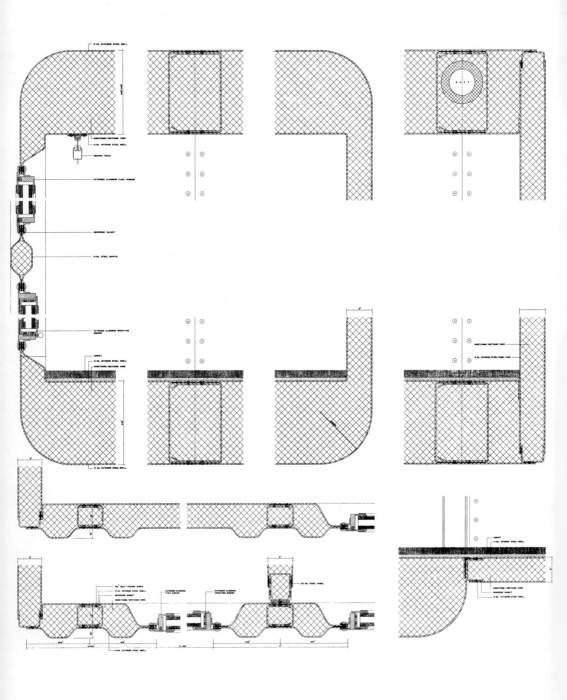

Facade sections with window and wall detail (urethane insulation).
144

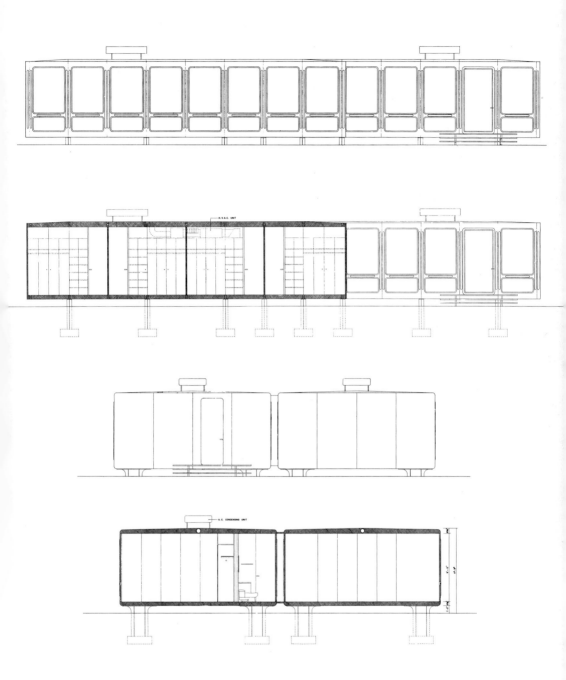

Elevations and sections of the one-story house.

Collage study with works by Picasso and Miró
showing alternative use of the space as a gallery.
147

Buildings by Mies, 1939–69

Mies used to say: 'Structure is a constructional form of correlated work, a uniform system, a design lucidly pursued to its end in every detail.' To the dictum 'Form follows function' ascribed to Louis Sullivan, Mies opposed the concept of structural design. The functions in a building may change but its form remains. A structure of frame and infill embodies a principle which also allows changing needs to be met. This is an essential tenet of what he taught and he constantly gave it material form in his buildings.

At Mies' office in Ohio Street the model workshop was important. The volume of the building was evolved in the model, incorporated in the immediate environment of the site, and adapted to it. Studies of the details of the construction and the rhythm of the facade design were also worked out on the model. The final result could be tested for rationality and economy only when represented in drawings. This work was done over many years by Mies' students. Instruction and practice were one. Mies said: 'Architecture occurs where purposes are realized in structure. The intent to limit oneself to one structure is not a restriction but also an aid.' Often Mies initiated his ideas with his students at IIT and then continued and completed them at his office.

The buildings shown here are not in chronological order, nor are they complete; they serve the purpose of clearly showing the principles on which Mies deployed the construction. After 1940 the first of the classroom and laboratory buildings of IIT were built; the great hall of the Department of Architecture in their center was added in 1950–56. The tower block on Lake Michigan, 1948–51, was the prototype for many successors. In the downtown area (Loop) the complex of the Federal Center, 1959–73, comprises buildings grouped round a sculpture by Calder, 1974. This was one of the last projects by Mies, the Post Office in steel and glass being completed by his successors (Office of Mies van der Rohe, now FCL) in accordance with his ideas. These textbook examples of high-rise buildings on the principle of the skeleton and curtain wall serve to show with particular clarity how decisively the whole and the detail determine each other. Unless the order of the whole is visible in the detail, the whole is not in order. It is only within a lucid system in which the various requirements of purpose, material, space and modes of construction are coordinated that proportions, rhythms and colors can be modulated with imagination.

Illinois Institute of Technology Campus (IIT),
Chicago 1939–58

General considerations
After Mies van der Rohe had been commissioned
with the building of the new Institute of Technology in Chicago in 1939, he gave this task priority of
attention. Mies said in 1955: 'The Illinois Institute
of Technology was the biggest decision I ever had
to make. We began to build more than fifteen years
ago and everything should be finished by now –
but, of course, it will take another ten years. Once a
single building has been built, you can leave it
standing and walk away. But today 25 years is a
long time and I knew that our way of building had
to outlast this spell without getting outdated.'

Spatial organization
The campus of Illinois Institute of Technology
is constructed on a 24-foot grid which determines
all the elements of the project. The IIT commission
was relatively uncomplicated: the individual laboratory and classroom blocks had to be erected on a
street grid in such a way that they could be built to
meet specific requirements and yet continue to
form a harmonious whole throughout the long
period of construction. The solution to the problem
was found in a dispersed system of pavilions, not of
the closely-meshed kind in which temporary needs
are satisfied directly but rather in a spacious system
of coordinations in which each building receives its
due measure.

Technical development
The buildings of the Institute are framed in reinforced concrete or steel. The bearing elements of
the multifloor buildings are fireproofed with reinforced concrete and are set back from the facade.
The system of construction is not subject to any
hard-and-fast rules; rather is the load-bearing
skeleton in each building amenable to flexible use
and developed according to the changing spatial
structure – two- or three-story blocks – and also in
the form of hall constructions for open-plan
designs. Extreme economy had to be observed in
carrying out this project.

Aesthetic considerations
The existing street grid is embodied in the campus.
Dispersed verdant zones, planted with acacia trees,
are broken up by walks. Thus the groups of buildings are harmonized with nature. The principle of
order with the strict organization of the buildings
and the sparing use of verdant zones results in a
design which is lucid in terms of city planning. The
campus is characterized by three main building
materials: black painted steel, glass, and pearly
gray brickwork.
Mies scaled his campus buildings entirely to man.
Only in recent years have these buildings shown to
full advantage in all their beauty as growing nature
has enfolded them. For Mies architecture is not so
much the 'queen of the arts' as the 'servant of life'.
150

150–161

Illinois Institute of Technology (IIT) Chicago, Campus buildings 1939–56, Mies van der Rohe, Chicago.

Open-house exhibition of students' work together with projects by Mies 1951 in the Alumni Memorial Hall, 1945–46, then used as the Faculty of Architecture Building.

151

The avenue between the buildings is incorporated
into the 24-foot grid. In the background the Alumni Memorial Hall.

Chemical Engineering and Metallurgy Building
(two stories) and Chemistry Building (three
stories), 1945–46. The campus area is planted with
acacia trees.

Student Commons Building, 1952–53. Steel skeleton with brick infill.
155

Crown Hall (IIT), Chicago 1950–56

General considerations
The projects for large one-room buildings, Crown
Hall at IIT and the National Theater in Mannheim, took shape at about the same time in the fifties and were handled by students at IIT and in
Mies' office. The building at IIT comprised a simple large room without columns whereas a still
vaster and more complex suite of rooms was
developed under a single roof for the Mannheim
Theater. As with all Mies' basic ideas, these projects can be traced back to precursors in earlier
years, for example, when the collage for a concert
hall, sketches for a museum for a small city, and
the Cantor drive-in restaurant were created. But
only Crown Hall and, years later, the New
National Gallery in Berlin were built.

Spatial organization
Crown Hall is the building for the Department of
Architecture, City and Regional Planning and also
houses the Institute of Design. The roof is suspended from four steel girders. The hall itself, a
very large room enclosed by low walls, accommodates the drafting area and a small administrative
office. In the basement are the workshops, class-
rooms, cloakrooms and washing facilities. Instruction of the 400 or so students forming all the classes
of the Faculty of Architecture takes place in the
glazed hall. It is subdivided only by low partitions
which separate the various classes yet facilitate
communication between them. On these walls
hang the latest plans, which are intended to stimu-
late discussion, rather like the poster walls in modern China. The aims of teaching and learning –
which are visually incorporated in the room – are
thus the subject of a lively dialogue between teachers and students, and among the students themselves. Such close contact in this fascinating hall
where the wall display stimulates discussion helps
to keep teaching vital.

Technical development
The roof of Crown Hall is suspended from four
steel girders with a span of 120 feet supported on 8
external steel columns. The columns are set at
60-foot centers and the roof projects 20 feet at the
ends. The whole glass-and-steel external wall gains
from the severity of the geometrical pattern Mies
imposed upon it.

Aesthetic considerations
The basic principle of Crown Hall is of particular
interest. This elongated glass structure was deliberately developed as a utility building capable of
being adapted to any other function at a later date.
The entire outer wall consists of fixed glass. All external steel is painted charcoal black. The lower
portion of the large glass plates is of translucent
glass up to door level. There are light-colored
venetian blinds behind the glass and the internal
partitions are of natural oak.
156

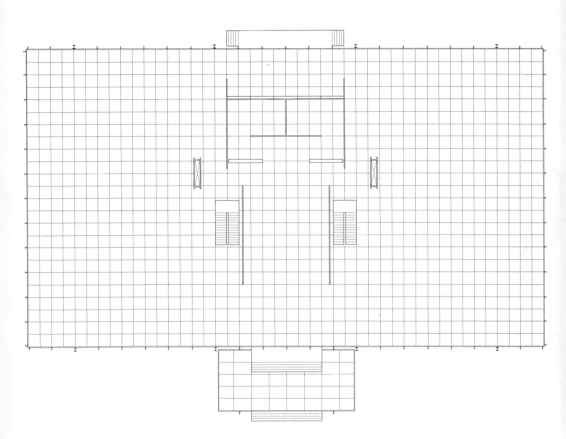

156–161

Crown Hall (College of Architecture, Planning and Design), IIT, 1950–56, Mies van der Rohe, Chicago. (Associate architects: Pace Associates.)

Plan of the building with large column-free interior, $\frac{1}{40}'' = 1'0''$

157

The roof of Crown Hall is carried by 4 plate girders spanning 120 feet on columns spaced 60 feet
apart. (The hall had no internal venetian blinds
when this photograph was taken in 1974.)
159

Free-standing partition walls in the hall were used
during the summer months (1963) for an open-
house exhibition of the students' work. The large
room (classroom for the Department of Architecture) measures 120×220 feet and is 18 feet high.
161

860–880 Lake Shore Drive Apartments,
Chicago 1948–51

General considerations
The Promontory Apartments in Chicago, built in
1946–49, were Mies' first tower apartment blocks.
They are concrete frame constructions with a brick
infill. In a study he suspended a curtain wall of
steel and glass. This version was the actual precur-
sor of the trend-setting and epoch-making 860–880
Lake Shore Drive Apartments. Today the two
apartment towers of steel and glass are placed
somewhat in the shade by the high-rise blocks constructed since then. In the immediate vicinity, like
giant soaring staircases, stand the John Hancock
Building and others. Yet the Lake Shore Drive
Apartments, with their simple steel skeleton construction, hold their own against the formal chaos
of many of the neighboring skyscrapers.

Spatial organization
The two identical 26-story apartment towers of
glass and steel stand in close association with the
900 Esplanade Apartments, also built by
Mies in 1956, in the most attractive part of Chicago
by Lake Michigan close to the 'Loop' business
center. They are the first fully-glazed detached
skyscrapers with a skeleton frame.

Technical development
During the construction of the facade one four-
window unit at a time was assembled on the roof
and then lowered and fixed from column to
column at 21-foot centers. On the columns and corner pillars, which are fireproofed with concrete and
covered with steel plates, are welded the same continuous vertical standard I-beam sections as make
up the window units. On this point Mies said: 'It
was very important to maintain the rhythm of the
steel I-beam mullions which dominate the whole
building and to carry them through consistently.
We looked at the problem on the model and the
building did not look complete without the
I-beams placed in front of the columns. At the
same time these mullions served to stiffen the
covers of the columns so that they did not buckle
and also helped to give rigidity to the window-unit
assemblies.'

Aesthetic considerations
The steel construction, which runs the full height of
the glazed facade, stands out in black against the
uniformly gray curtains and aluminum windows.
Another dictum of Mies: 'Our imagination went
into the construction. We did not use our ideas for
the form but for the structural possibilities.'

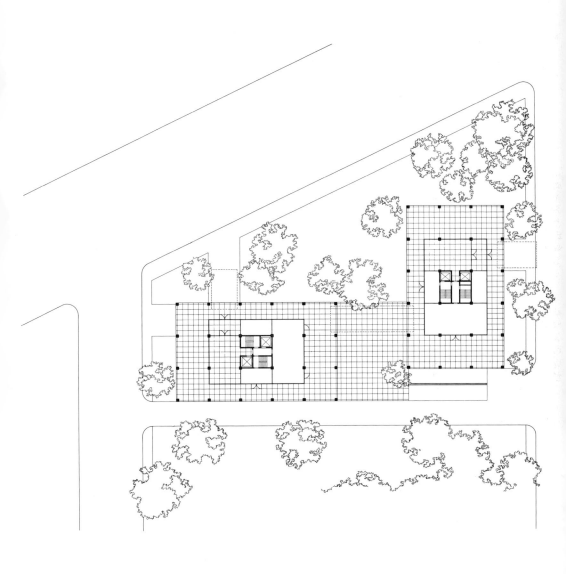

162-171

860-880 Lake Shore Drive Apartments, Chicago,
1948-51, Mies van der Rohe, Chicago.
(Associate architects: Pace Associates and Holsman, Holsman, Klekamp and Taylor.)

General plan. Two identical 26-story towers, 40
feet apart, by Lake Michigan, $\frac{1}{64}'' = 1'0''$.

163

Mies shows masterly skill in inserting a building
into an existing street facade: the glass skyscraper
on a prismatic plan in the Bahnhof-Friedrich-
strasse in Berlin, 1919 (p. 164), and the delicately
articulated apartment block in East Chestnut Street
on Lake Shore Drive in Chicago, 1951 (p. 165).

165

The canopy connecting the two apartment towers.
Integration of building and landscape.

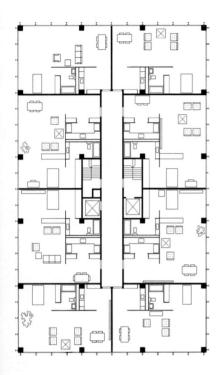

One-room plan (not executed), $\frac{1}{32}'' = 1'0''$. The
columns are 21 feet apart.

The complex of apartment blocks on Lake Michigan
fits harmoniously into the Chicago skyscraper
silhouette. (900 Esplanade Apts. on right)

The two towers each of 26 stories are set back on a trapezoidal lot. This first steel-and-glass skyscraper with 'Chicago' windows is already part of architectural history.

171

Prefabricated Robert McCormick House, Elmhurst (Illinois), 1951–52

General considerations

Today nobody talks about the McCormick House, whereas the project attracted keen attention when it was realized in the fifties. Mies' idea was to use elements of existing facade units in order to develop a low-cost prefabricated house. However, although the prototype was a success, production on an industrial scale never materialized. The position is quite different with the Farnsworth House at Plano, which was built at about the same time, changed owners in the seventies, and is today a 'Mies Museum' containing his classical furniture. It is, however, questionable whether this renovation is in accordance with Mies' principles, for he had originally intended for this house simple furniture from the context of sport and recreation.

Spatial organization

The house (a factory prototype for Robert McCormick, the promoter of the Lake Shore Drive Apartments) stands amidst a luxuriant park landscape and embodies the same steel frame construction as the two apartment houses on Lake Shore Drive. The McCormick house represents a further development from these basic elements and has been enlarged to form a Z-plan with a covered porch.

Technical development

The roof spans the whole distance from facade to facade and rests upon the facade frame, which is assembled in the workshop and erected on the site.

Aesthetic considerations

The narrow ends have a panel wall of pearl-gray brick. All steel parts are painted white, the curtains are of gray material, the doors are natural oak.

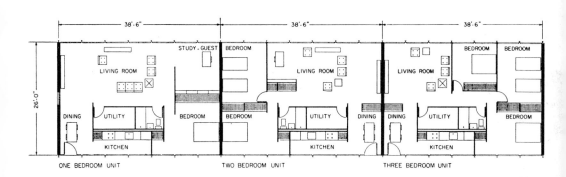

ONE BEDROOM UNIT   TWO BEDROOM UNIT   THREE BEDROOM UNIT

172–179

Robert McCormick House, Elmhurst (Illinois),
1951–52, Mies van der Rohe, Chicago.   Proposal for row houses.

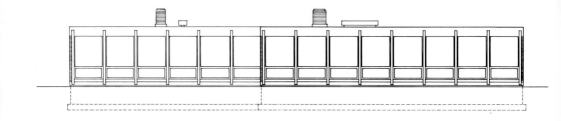

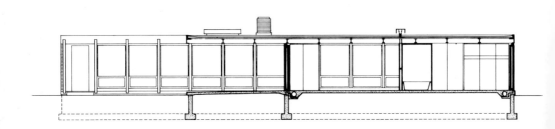

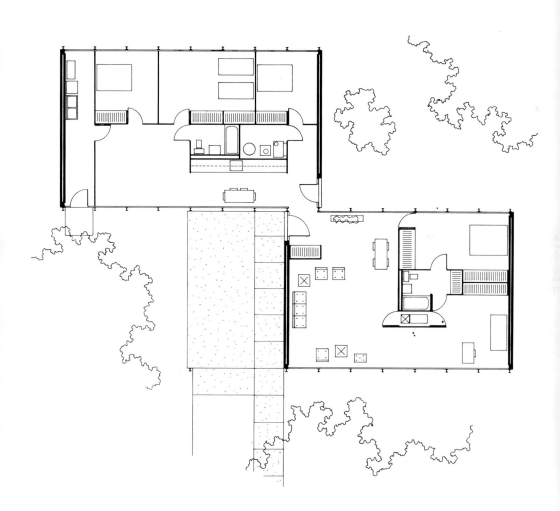

Two units (master bedroom-and-living room and
bedroom-and-dining room) form the house. Row
houses of the same units were also planned. Elevations, section and plan $\frac{1}{16}'' = 1'0''$.
175

The steel frame of 860 Lake Shore Drive Apartments is used for a prefabricated dwelling house. Roof view showing two standard elements joined together. Elevation with infill of pearl-gray brickwork.

177

The vertical steel I-beams are located in front of
the facade frame just as in the apartment blocks.
General view from the west. The unspoiled park
landscape becomes part of the home atmosphere.
179

Chicago Federal Center, 1959–73

General considerations

In the innermost core of Chicago, the business center known as the 'Loop', skyscrapers jostle side by side, and their number has increased since Mies' day. It was always Mies' endeavor to find a way of fitting the new into the existing townscape so as to achieve the subtlest integration. Back in the twenties Mies was known in Berlin for his skill in neatly dovetailing his glass skyscraper projects into the existing street facades. Even at that time these projects were notable for their novel glazed skeleton facades and their outstanding spatial organization. In the sixties this idea was developed in the Federal Center and acquired a still vaster scale. Mies inspired this piece of city planning through his principles but did not live to see it realized in its entirety by his school.

Spatial organization

By concentrating the building masses in two skyscrapers of 30 and 45 floors it was possible to give greater breadth to the densely built urban area at this point. The low building for the United States Post Office with a column-free interior of 197 feet square is glazed on all sides and set back from the street so that a plaza is formed. The glass fronts of the giant skyscrapers reflect each other. The 30-story building (Everett McKinley Dirksen Building, 219 South Dearborn Street) serves the Court and also as an office while the 45-floor high-rise building (Federal Building, 230 South Dearborn Street) was planned for offices.

Technical development

The two skyscrapers are steel skeleton constructions with fixed glazing, the columns being set back behind the curtain wall so that the glass fronts, reinforced with I-beam mullions, are erected at regular intervals round the building. As long ago as the twenties Mies had been interested in glass skyscrapers. 'I thought of the structural possibilities of glass and not of an expressionistic design. Reinforcing elements are needed to hold the glass. I moved these outside so as to obtain a front that is not dead.'

Aesthetic considerations

Externally the buildings look very dark with black steel frames and gray-tinted glass. A contrast to these is formed by Alexander Calder's 'Flamingo' a vermilion painted steel sculpture 54 feet high in a square frequented by many pedestrians. It soars above the one-story post office building.

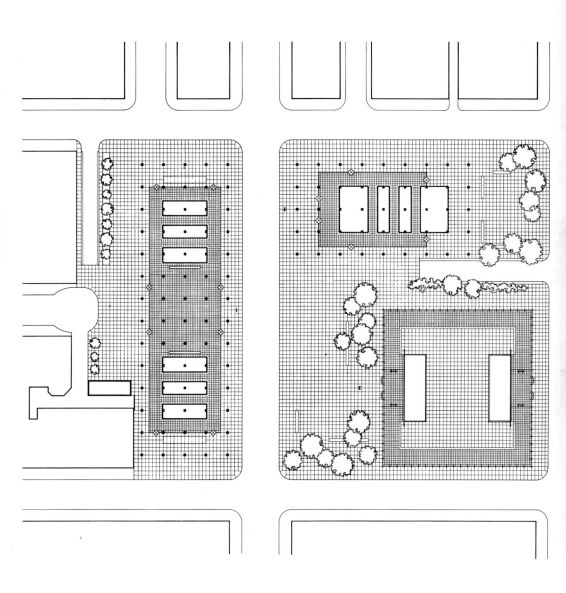

180–187

Federal Office Building Complex Chicago, 1959–73.
Mies van der Rohe, Chicago. (Associate architects
C.F. Murphy Assoc., Schmidt, Garden & Erikson,
A. Epstein and Sons Inc., Chicago.)

General plan (US Courthouse and Federal Office,
US Post Office Building).
181

The office towers on South Dearborn Street
(Loop), left the 30-story and right the 45-story
building.

The space between the three skeleton buildings:
views looking in, out and through.

The curtain-wall facade of the Federal Center and
in the foreground the steel construction of the Post
Office.
185

A steel sculpture 'Flamingo' by Alexander Calder
has been standing in the plaza in front of the building complex since 1974. The charcoal black steel
skeleton as a backdrop to the vermilion-colored
sculpture.
187

Concert Hall, project 1942

General considerations
Mies continually endeavored to define the idea of
structure by reference to the most varied examples:
'I tried to construct chairs with stiffening ribs out of
a mass like seashells. That is a mass and not a skeleton. I have not tried to make a structure into a
mass.'

Spatial organization
As a rule a well-proportioned room has good
acoustics. This view, which is held by leading con-
ductors, can be readily translated into architectural
reality by reason of the complete freedom Mies affords in the design of his column-free rooms. In
this one-room architecture with its wide span of
roof resting on external columns a concert hall can
be created by arranging wooden walls to enclose
the space like the walls of a resonance box. These
built-in elements are independent of the columns
and the roof. Mies explained this idea to me with
the aid of a freehand sketch in 1964 (Fig. 189).

Aesthetic considerations
Within the large room, represented by a collage
imposed on a photograph of Albert Kahn's interior
of the 'Martin Bomber Plant' near Baltimore, Mies
investigated the various possibilities of enclosing
the auditorium with screens. The horizontal wall
screen has been evolved in conformity with acous-
tic principles. Various materials were experimented
with for these wall screens. Under Mies' direction
IIT students worked on collages with wooden
screens of this kind and tried out solutions of primary and metallic colors. In the foreground stood
Aristide Maillol's sculpture 'La Méditerranée de
1900' whose rounded forms were intended as a foil
to the angular architecture.

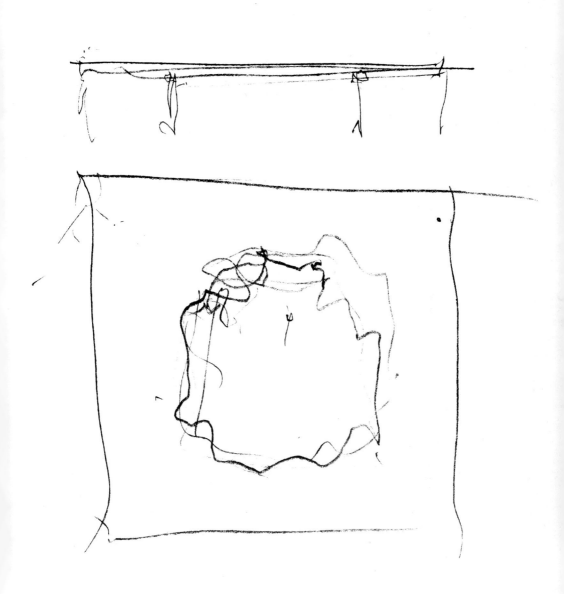

Quick sketch by Mies for a concert hall, done during a discussion in 1964.
189

Project for concert hall, collage with wood and low
metal and marble wall, 1942, Mies van der Rohe,
Chicago (and graduate study with Daniel Brenner).
191

Museum for a small city, project 1942

General considerations
This museum project ushered in a new way of ex-
hibiting and viewing works of art. The museum
was intended to contain rooms in which the works
needed to be neither hung nor 'stage set'. The room
and the works of art in it should form a unit which
transposes the viewer from the outside world into a
completely new atmosphere governed by mathe-
matical laws. Morever, the building should form a
harmonious contrast to the landscape surrounding
it. At IIT the design of a museum was a favorite
subject for graduate studies. The use of collage to
represent the works of art integrated with the room
was part of the project study. Often the corpus of
the building was surrounded by courtyards for the
display of sculptures. The interior of the building,
conceived as a large free area, could be altered at
will.

Spatial organization
Two apertures in the roof slab illuminate a small
interior court and a corridor at the end of the
building. The external walls and walls enclosing
the interior court consist entirely of glass. Three
freestanding wall screens form the auditorium. The
roof over the auditorium is suspended from two externally visible girders similar in type to those subsequently used in the hall constructions.

Technical development
With regard to this museum Mies said: 'The building, which is conceived as a single large surface, is
alterable by reason of the steel-frame construction.
The floor and terraces are of natural stone. The administrative offices are under the same roof but
separated from the exhibition room.'

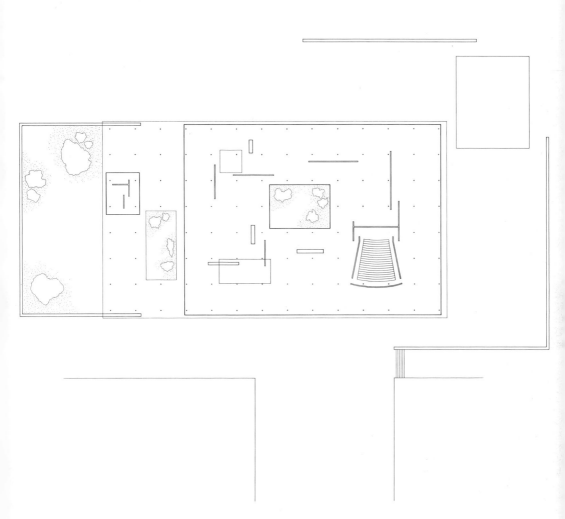

193–195

Project: Museum for a small city, 1942,
Mies van der Rohe, Chicago
(and graduate study with George Danforth).
193

The large open area in front of the museum is incorporated into the interior. Sketch by Mies.
195

Convention Hall, Chicago, project 1953–54

General considerations
In his catalogue for the Mies van der Rohe exhibition of 1968 at the Art Institute of Chicago, James Speyer wrote: 'In heroic scale and power of construction the Convention Hall leaves behind everything else 20th century architecture has produced. It is the ultimate in column-free rooms.' Since then, especially in recent years, members of the school of Mies, mainly the team of C.F. Murphy Assoc. have continued to develop this idea of the column-free interior in major projects outside Chicago.

Spatial organization
Mies worked on this idea for a large multipurpose hall to accommodate 50,000 persons as a co-operative project with his advanced students Pao-Chi Chang, Henry Kanazawa, and Yujiro Miwa. It forms a square with a side of 720 feet and no columns in the interior. This idea could be developed in either of two directions: in the direction of large-dimensioned air-conditioned rooms or in the direction of wide-spanned grid structures with a flexible interior finish.

Technical development
The roof is 30 feet high and consists of a framework of steel girders running in both directions and resting on an outer wall of 60-foot high steel trusses raised on all sides on concrete columns. Mies on architecture: 'Where large buildings took shape, such as industrial and transport buildings, the purpose was the actual designer and the construction was the means of realization.'

Aesthetic considerations
The load-bearing structure is visible everywhere inside and out. There are a number of variants with different infills. Mies explored the possibilities of aluminum sheets of various textures. The final variant consists of green marble slabs.

196–201

Project: Convention Hall for Chicago, 1953–54,
Mies van der Rohe, Chicago (and graduate study
Pao-chi Chang, Henry Kanazawa, Yujiro Miwa).   Model study of a variant construction.

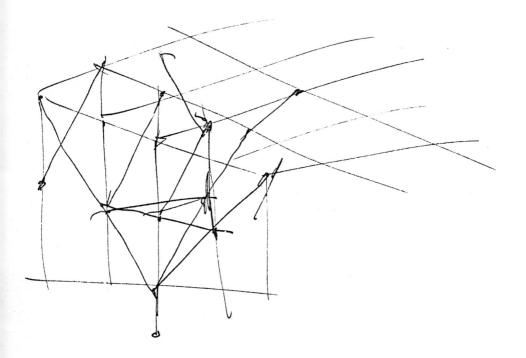

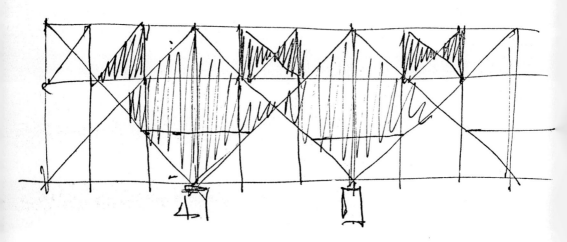

Sketch by Mies of the load-bearing structure,
30 feet high.

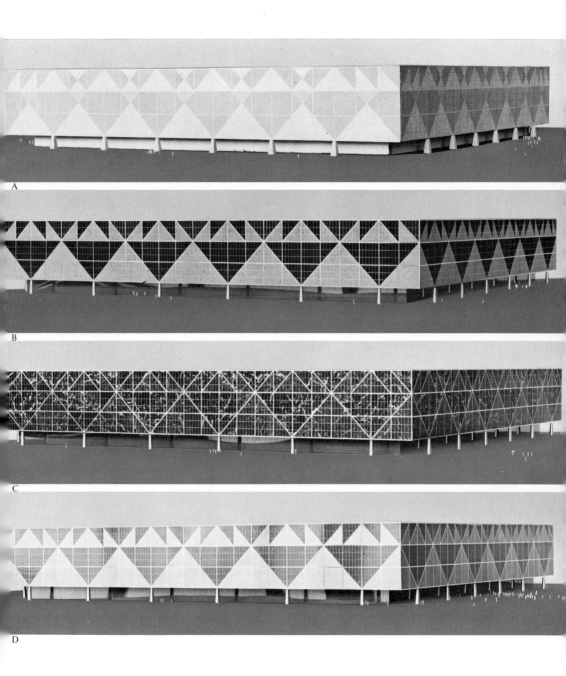

Study models:
(A) Non-subjective, good in warmer climate with colorful landscape. The earlier scheme 700 × 700 feet. Cream white, yellow in two tones and light gray marble for skin.
(B) 720 × 720 feet. Study of strong contrast, dark brown, black and tan granite as skin. Subjective.
(C) Classic look, 720 × 720 feet. Study of weak contrast. Green and black marble as skin.

(D) 720 × 720 feet, a building created by our technology, non-subjective. This was finally selected. Gray tones, metal panels as skin. Possibly aluminum insulated panels, with metal anodized to obtain different tones. All these were practical studies and did not obscure the structure but rather lent it greater emphasis. This one, however, was finally chosen since it goes with the steel structure and is not subjective.

199

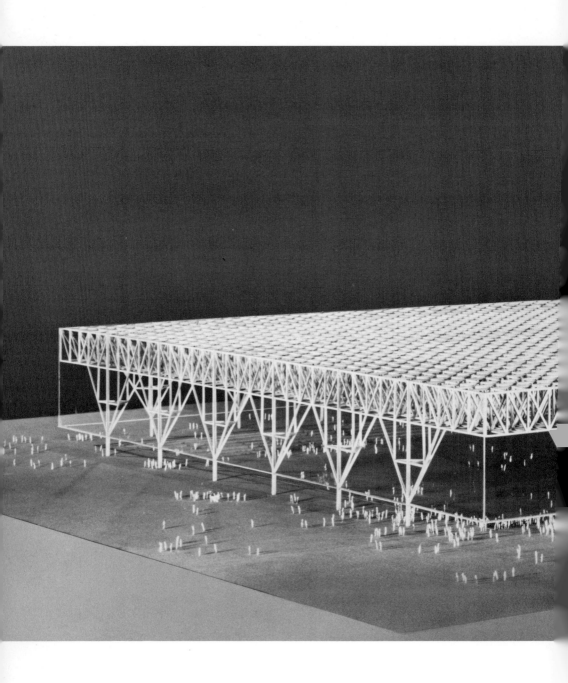

Studies to elucidate size with the aid of a model.

New National Gallery, Berlin 1962–68

General considerations
Is it not a curious dispensation of fate that, at the
end of his career, Mies was able to create a particularly impressive work again in Berlin? The building
is, admittedly, often questioned as a museum. But
for Mies himself it was primarily a matter of creat-
ing a prestigious hall construction which could be
used for various purposes. In his preliminary projects he worked with his students on collages and
models with a view to establishing agreement and
harmony between the work of art and space.

Spatial organization
The large square hall is oriented along one axis
towards the dainty Church of St. Matthew, which
was alone left standing in this area after the war.
On the large open terrace, ornamented with sculptures, rises the giant steel construction with the
column-free glass pavilion which is set back. Of
this building Mies said: 'The Berlin museum had
to have a monumental form and we therefore set
the hall on a terrace. This idea was prompted by
the inclination of the land, and to prevent this being seen from the outside, we have put a wall
around.' In the basement, which houses the permanent collection, the front faces the sculpture
court. Here the usual suite of small exhibition
rooms is broken up by wide vistas which at the
same time concentrate attention on special relationships between pictures.

Technical development
The roof, which measures 214 feet square, is a steel
structural grid made up of square modules 12 feet
long and 6'2" deep. It rests on eight cruciform steel
columns. The elements in the interior faced with
green Tinos marble have no load-bearing function.
They serve for ventilation and to drain the roof.

Aesthetic considerations
The surfaces for hanging pictures consist of wall
elements freely suspended from the ceiling. White
curtains regulate the daylight on three sides. The
hall is illuminated with warm diffuse light from a
lighting system set in the egg-crate roof which allows a variety of combinations for travelling exhibitions.

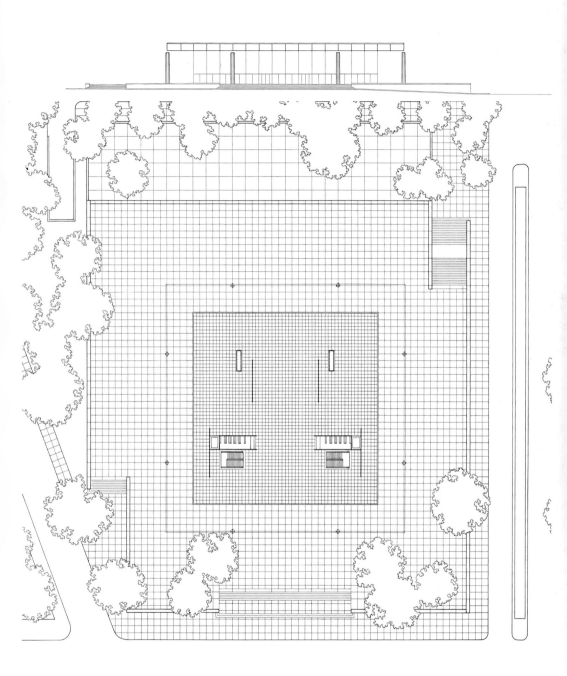

202–209

New National Gallery in Berlin, 1962–68,
Mies van der Rohe, Chicago.

Plan of upper floor and view into the basement
with sculpture courtyard.
203

Presentation of works of art in the hall surrounded
by two marble-faced columns and light glass partition walls, Mondrian exhibition on the occasion of
the opening in 1969.

Entrance with Barcelona furniture and transparent
steel-and-glass construction.

Square roof slab with a side of 64.80 meters
(214 feet) and recessed glass enclosure. Sculptures
are set out on the large platform; in the background can be seen St. Matthew's and Scharoun's
Philharmonie Building.

Cruciform column with heavy steel architrave and
egg-crate roof.

Granite slabs 1.20×1.20 meters (building module
3′11″) pave the floor of the open area and the interior.
The architecture is governed inside and outside by
the same idea. The steel sculpture 'Têtes et Queue'
by Alexander Calder dates from 1965.

Buildings by former students, 1961–81

The school of Mies can be understood in terms of his principles, his works, and his students' interpretation of them. For Mies the principles he taught and building were one. It is now the task of the students to develop solutions of their own out of this unity while making due allowance for present conditions. On my visit to Chicago in November 1974 the successors of Mies showed me the ideas and projects evolved in the years following his death. Besides their practical activities many of these ex-students also work as teachers at IIT. As in earlier days ideas are developed at IIT and then subsequently find expression in Chicago in practical applications. For this reason Chicago is still today a treasure trove for architects. What was begun in the Chicago School of Architecture at the end of the last century and reformulated by Mies in 1938 is now being continued by his successors as a Second Chicago School of Architecture. Although the Miesian concern with detail and the travertine marble he favored are to be found everywhere in Chicago, it would be wrong to talk of imitation.

The John Heinrich House outside Chicago has no doubt a character of its own but the Miesian principles are unmistakably there. In the program for eduction at IIT the courtyard house still occupies a very important place.

This idea in Chicago was first realized in the works of Y. C. Wong, an architect from China, who continued his training at IIT and then built atrium houses in Chicago. Later David Haid planned courtyard houses as redevelopment projects. In Chicago and the surrounding region there are numerous large buildings which show the consistency and precision of Mies. I have taken pictures of some of these examples so that they can be compared with buildings by Mies himself I have also photographed. Mies said: 'Building has obviously less to do with the invention of new forms than with the organization in a construction of the clearly defined relationships between things. Our efforts are directed more and more towards an objective architecture supported by constructional ideas which find their expression in a clear structure.'

Dwelling house at Barrington Hills (Illinois),
by John C. Heinrich, under construction

General considerations
For more than a century Chicago has enjoyed the
reputation of being the citadel of architecture. The
buildings of the downtown business center of the
city with its skyscrapers are known in the jargon as
'The Loop Chicago School of Architecture', and
the villas in the region are called 'The Prairie
Chicago School of Architecture'. The two architects
Schipporeit and Heinrich, both students of Mies,
built the striking example of Lake Point Tower
Apartments, a glass skyscraper on a polygonal plan,
in Chicago in 1968 (p. 224–227).
Mies taught that a knowledge of materials was of
the most elementary importance but not so much
from an aesthetic point of view. How to handle
materials was something which was much better
learned on a building site. The process of building
itself was the guide. Tutored in these elementary
principles the students of Mies had no difficulty in
putting up a building themselves (as owner, architect, and builder in one) and in solving the problems by their own experimentation. It is obvious
that the builder will not complicate his open questions unnecessarily and will thus arrive at simple
practical solutions in the choice of material and
construction. Heinrich teaches at IIT and it will
therefore be appreciated that many students wel-
comed an opportunity to help in the building during their free time. Theory and building practice
are closely linked and provide a splendid basis on
which to understand the work of the teacher.

Spatial organization and aesthetic considerations
In the John Heinrich House at Barrington Hills,
a long-term project (because of the amount
of work the constructor is doing himself), there
are brick walls which project into the natural surroundings, a characteristic feature of the school of
Mies. The roof slab rests on the load-bearing pearl-
gray brickwork which determines the character of
the building. The flowing transition of the living
areas into one another and the interior location of
the services area brings a great deal of freedom
into the plan. Heinrich's mastery in handling the
brick walls, guided by a highly sophisticated sense
of proportion, comes very clearly to light in this
textbook example.

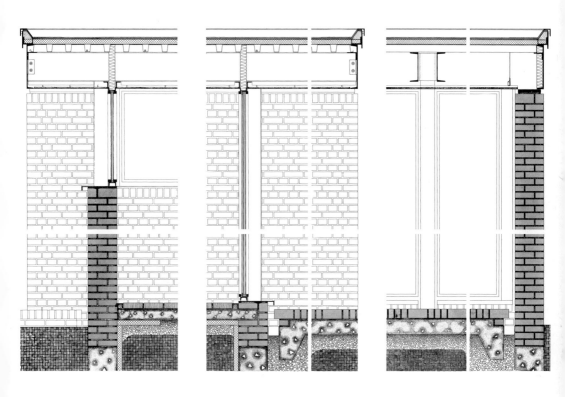

212–217

John Heinrich's own house at Barrington Hills
(Illinois), under construction since 1970.

Vertical section of the wall and facade construction. Mies' principles have been taken a stage further without detracting from the basic idea.

213

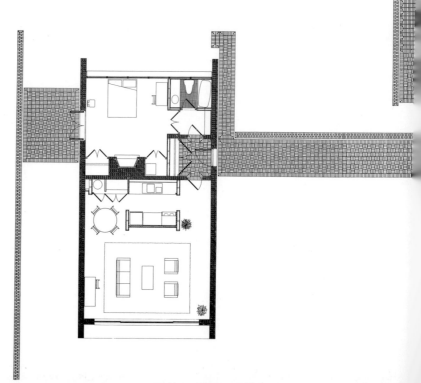

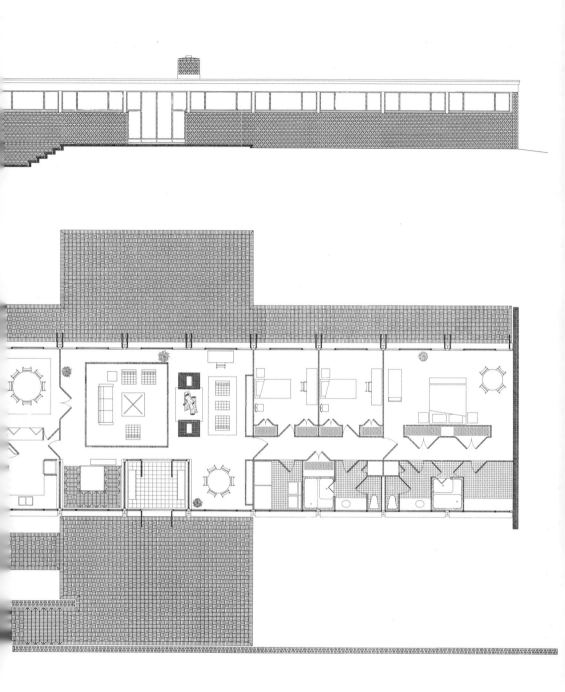

Plan and elevation of dwelling and guesthouse.
215

Guesthouse with elemental brick construction set
in the landscape. An ideal building material with
respect to compressive strength, warmth, sound insulation. No facing is required.

217

Atrium houses, Hyde Park, Chicago,
by Y.C. Wong, 1961

General considerations
The atrium house is of particular importance in the
curriculum of IIT during the 3rd and 4th years of
study. Starting with a simple plan the student has
to learn to place walls and to control their three-
dimensional interpenetration into external space.
This is practised with great precision on a scale
model $\frac{1}{4}'' = 1'0''$ (p.68). At the same time material
and construction, which together with spatial
arrangement form the main factor in this work,
are also clarified.

Spatial organization
It was only in 1961 that Y.C. Wong was afforded
an opportunity to build houses on the atrium principle in Chicago. Perhaps the fact that it was an architect from China who was the first to build such
houses is not unconnected with the importance of
the courtyard house in Ancient China. For centu-
ries noblemen in Peking built homes which present
only a wall to the street but open inside onto one or
more courtyards. Surprisingly teaching at IIT has
never taken cognizance of these interesting examples. The atrium houses by Y.C. Wong stand half-
way between the Chinese houses and those of the
school of Mies. Some are single-story houses with
an atrium while others are two-story buildings with
a forecourt and others again three-story row
houses. In every case the brick wall enclosing the
court creates a private sphere. They are in principle
simple dwelling houses which can be arranged by
their inhabitants to suit their needs. Here again the
structural principle allows changes to be made in
the interior.

Aesthetic considerations
The walls enclosing the forecourts and the infills of
the two-story houses are of light brown engineering
brick. The structural steelwork is visible in the interior while floor-to-ceiling sliding glass doors
bring the walled garden visually into the living
room.

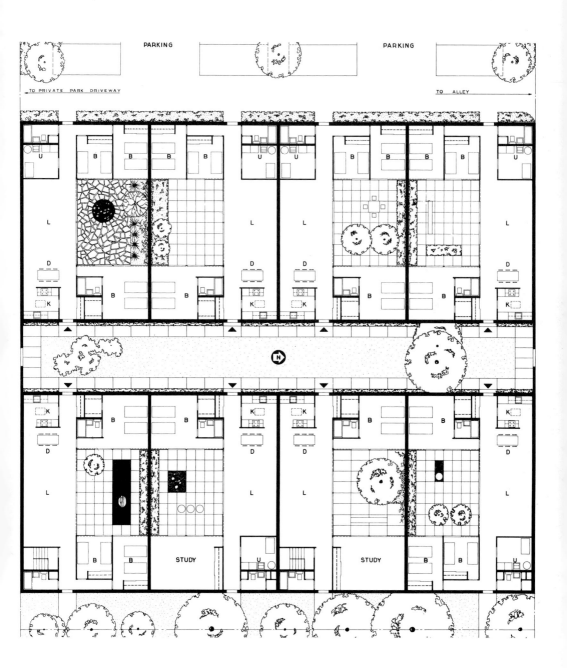

218–221

Atrium houses, Hyde Park, Chicago,
by Y. C. Wong, 1961.

Site plan: 8 houses with walled gardens.
Plan of ground and upper floor.

219

View from inside the house looking into the courtyard.

Privacy is ensured by the courtyard.

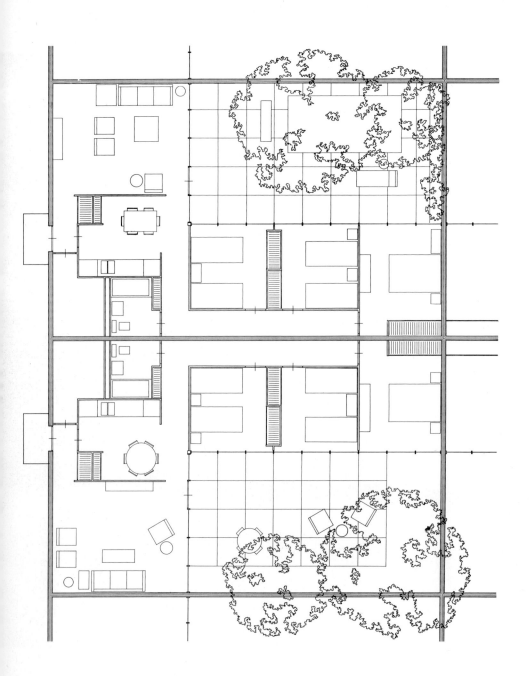

222–223

Proposed redevelopment plan with courtyard
houses (Chicago), by David Haid, 1967.

Model with one-story buildings (living area with
court approximately 1400 square feet).

Lake Point Tower, Chicago,
by George Schipporeit and John C. Heinrich,
1965–68

General considerations
The principles of Mies are also embodied in the
buildings of the past. The school of Mies realized
that it has not to utilize its knowledge for historical
reasons but out of its constant commitment to the
present. It is not therefore a question of discovering
new elements of design but rather of taking full advantage of technical possibilities in building. According to Mies, form is the result of a purely structural solution, structure being the essence of architecture.

Spatial organization
The triangular plan of the lower apartment block
on Lake Michigan is entirely suited to the situation: two fronts face the lake and the third front
the high-rise buildings from the pioneering days of
the Loop and Michigan Avenue. In front of the
building is an underground car park over which is
laid out a garden with a sheet of water, a playground and a lawn, designed by Alfred Caldwell.

Technical development
The synthesis achieved between the statics of the
structure and the dynamics of the facade design is
visible in Schipporeit's and Heinrich's 65-story
Lake Point Tower Apartments in Chicago. The organic curtain wall appears to be in motion round
the massive reinforced concrete columns. In their
basic design the architects were anxious to avoid
uneconomical corner details and to use a single
window unit. A partial air-conditioning system
could be installed because of the cool air of the
lake front. The glazing is of bronze-colored insulat-
ing glass and frames of gold-anodized aluminum
sections with the vertical component strongly
stressed by means of stiffening I-section mullions.

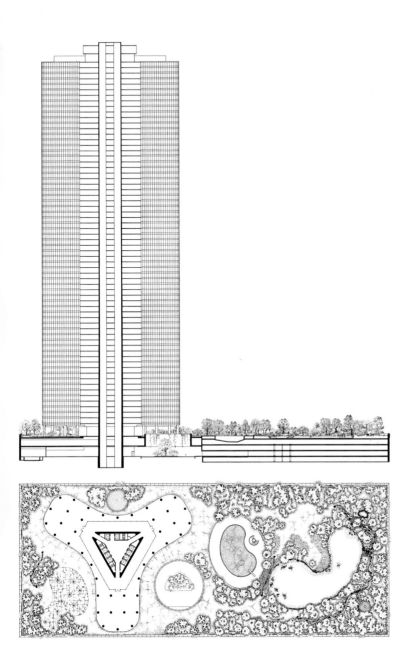

224–227

Lake Point Tower Chicago, 1965–68,
Schipporeit and Heinrich Assoc.,
Graham, Anderson, Probst and White, associate
architects.

Site plan with gardens by Alfred Caldwell.

High-rise apartment block of reinforced concrete
645 feet high with 883 apartments in Chicago's
premier residential district (Navy Pier, Lake Michigan and Lake Shore Drive).

The outer skin comprising concave and convex surfaces is placed in front of the columns.

Chicago Civic Center,
by Jacques C. Brownson, 1963–66

General considerations
One of Mies' most gifted pupils, Jacques C. Brownson, was given an opportunity to build a Civic Center for Chicago as a member of the Office of C.F. Murphy Assoc. The architect was aware of the great responsibility of respecting the heritage of the century-old tradition of the Chicago School of Architecture. This movement places its main emphasis on variation. It is inexhaustible in its constructional inspirations. The 'Loop' in Chicago is in this respect distinguished by other good examples of the school of Mies. Apart from the originals by Mies this design by Brownson is one of the most convincing because the large scale, which was always Mies' aim, stands out prominently in this building. Its generous and spacious layout can be adapted at any time to whatever uses are required. This building is indissolubly attached to Mies' conception and yet the building program is interpreted in an entirely novel way. The oft repeated criticism of the school of Mies that everything looks the same is quite unwarranted. Naturally, the basic structural character of the building looks monotonous to the beholder, but if he examines the careful detailing he will see that each building has its own personal character. What appears to be uniform from outside discloses a great creative diversity inside.

Technical development
In terms of city planning the all-glazed building of 31 stories 647 feet in height with four vertical cruciform columns on each front and externally visible horizontal steel grid strips (structural bay 87×48 feet) fits very well into the street facade. The wide spans are motivated by the desire for maximum variability needed, for example, for court rooms two stories in height. The building contains 120 court rooms with offices and ancillary rooms and also a cafeteria.

Aesthetic considerations
The steel skeleton of this skyscraper is of non-rusting Cor-Ten steel, i.e. a non-painted steel which acquires a protective layer of corrosion due to a non-soluble process of oxidation. In recent years it has become a tradition in Chicago to create a plaza in front of very large buildings and to erect there a striking work by a distinguished sculptor. The cubistic interpretation of a woman's head by Pablo Picasso, made of the same Cor-Ten steel as the structure, is splendidly adapted to the plaza and the building. Here again the combination of art and architecture for which Mies also strove has established a fashion.

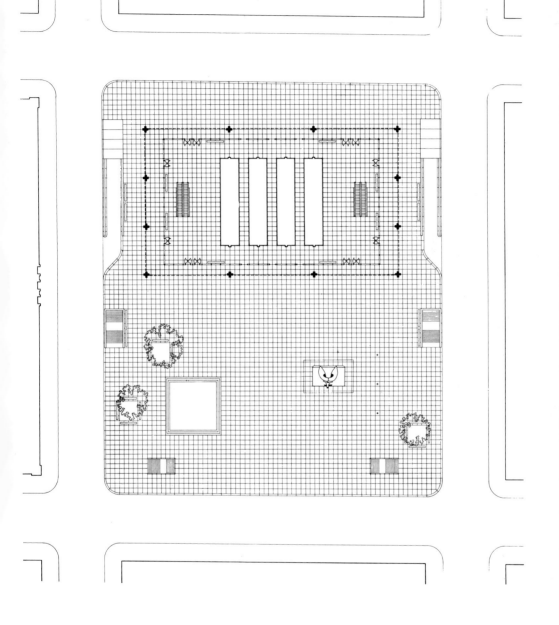

228–235

Chicago Civic Center, 1963–66.
Architect-in-charge Jacques C. Brownson
(C.F. Murphy Assoc., Skidmore, Owings and Merrill, Loeb, Schlossman, Bennett and Dart, Chicago).

General site plan between Clark and Dearborn
Street.
229

In the center of the Loop the Civic Center Plaza
with Picasso's sculpture of the Magical Woman's
Head in front of the skeleton structure of the building. Both in Cor-Ten steel.
231

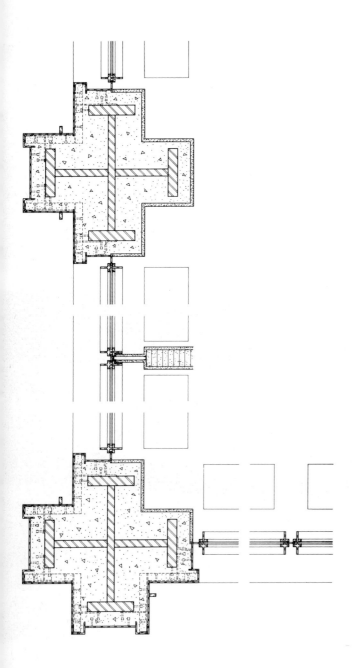

Horizontal section of typical columns and
windows.

Variant form of the spacious Chicago construction.
Corner showing the cruciform column and the pattern of the spandrels.

The length of the bay (87 feet) affords maximum
variability in the interior. Warren trusses 5'4" deep
were required.
235

McCormick Place-on-the-Lake, Chicago,
by Gene Summers,
1968–71

General considerations
Gene Summers was a close collaborator of Mies
for 16 years, particularly on large projects. As head
of the office he always had an insight into the
whole range of the master's work. On his first independent job with C.F. Murphy Assoc., the design
of a large exhibition and congress hall, he was able
to give scope to his talent for handling 'universal
space'. As everyone knows, Mies created the Convention Hall project of 1953 for a nearby site. It is
very interesting to compare the planned project
and the building that was actually constructed. Almost twenty years separate Mies' project study and
Summers' present building. During this period
technology has made great strides and offers entirely new possibilities for exhibition halls.

Spatial organization
The building executed is an enormous structure
under one roof comprising the large exhibition
area and the separate concert and congress hall.
Preliminary projects show these functions analyzed
into well-marked groups of buildings which are
better suited to the terrain. Unfortunately the client
did not accept these promising preliminaries, and
the building finally chosen appears to crowd the
site. Gene Summers concentrated his skill on the
construction and made a highly successful job of it.

Technical development
The exhibition hall is a vast room covering some
300,000 square feet with only eight columns. These
are cruciform, 5 feet in size, and arranged in both
directions 150 feet apart. The roof construction of
McCormick Place is 15 feet deep and consists of a
grid structure of lattice girders crossing at right an-
gles.

Aesthetic considerations
The building displays the high standard of 'Miesian details'. The structural steelwork is painted
black and the brickwork left exposed. The large-
scale steel skeleton and its glass enclosure are
linked to the open area of the terrace and the
broad lake promenade.

236–245

McCormick Place-on-the-Lake, Chicago
(Convention and Exhibition Center), 1968–71.
Architect-in-charge Gene Summers
(C.F. Murphy Assoc., Chicago).

The massing of the building and the landscape are
closely studied with the aid of a model (first version
not executed).
237

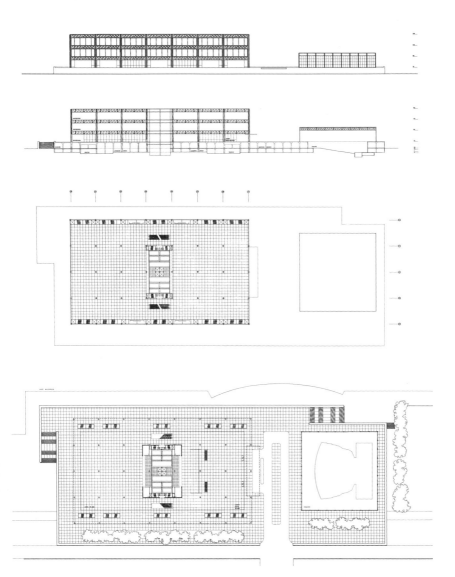

Plans of first version, divided into groups of buildings. The square concert hall is notable for its clear
construction and the free organic wall design.

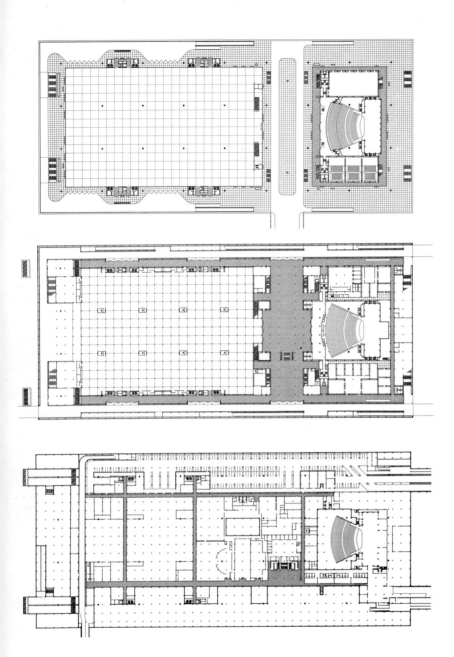

Plan of the hall at main floor level with an exhibition area of 300,000 square feet (final design).

The roof structure about 15 feet in depth, during
erection.

241

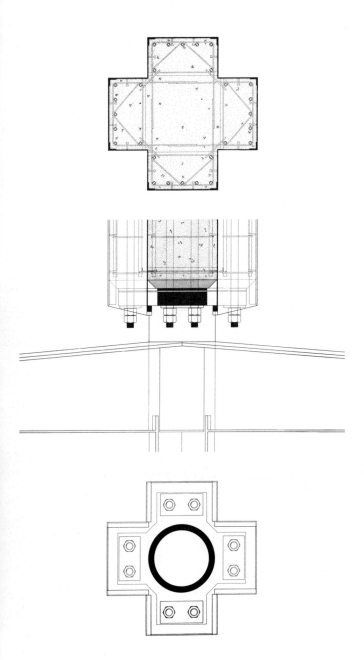

The columns are fireproofed with concrete covered
by a steel sheath.

The huge roof construction 1350 × 750 feet cantilevered to a distance of 75 feet is 115 feet above lake level.

243

Stairway faced in travertine marble leads down to
underground parking.

The roof construction comprises trussed girders
with columns spaced 150 feet apart.

Wendell Smith Elementary School, Chicago,
by Arthur Takeuchi, 1972–73

General considerations
Some important individual buildings by students
designed on the open-plan principle of Jacques
Brownson 1968–73 as head of the Public Building
Commission of Chicago were constructed by the
school of Mies: the Walter H. Dyett Middle School
by David Haid, the Keerfoot Vincennes Elementary School by Y.C. Wong, the Wendell Smith
Elementary School by Arthur Takeuchi, West Side
Community College, Malcolm X College and College of the Page by C.F. Murphy Assoc., and also
the Roberto Clemente High School, New Orr High
School and The New Loop College by the Office of
Mies van der Rohe, now FCL. Many of the school
buildings, unfortunately, were damaged by rebel-
lious youth during the disturbed 70's. The large
glazed openings had to be replaced by smaller ones
of plastic glass which are highly reflective and
make photography difficult.

Spatial organization
The school by Arthur Takeuchi, accommodating
1000 pupils ranging from kindergarten to the
eighth grade, is a two-story building round a courtyard which is used here as a playground. Already
in the buildings and projects of IIT (campus) there
were enclosed courts for light, air and planting. Arthur Takeuchi took up this idea and created an interior landscape which is beautifully organized spa-
tially.

Technical development
Arthur Takeuchi explains: 'The building structure
is a simple one-way system of truss girders and
joists supported on standard fireproof steel-clad
pipe columns spaced 30 feet apart. Within a relatively thin sandwich, this structural system readily
accommodates the necessary ducts, piping and fire
protection sprinkler lines. Fire-resistive acoustical
ceiling serves as the structure fireproofing.'

Aesthetic considerations
The model study looked particularly attractive by
reason of the white color of the facade contrasting
with the multicolored treatment of the interior
walls. As executed the building was painted black
throughout (because of the anticipated damage
and the impure air). The building has therefore lost
a great deal of its crispness. Even so, the integration of construction, space and proportion make
the Wendell Smith Elementary School an excellent
example of school building which, with its open
and closed plan, can still find many applications in
the future.

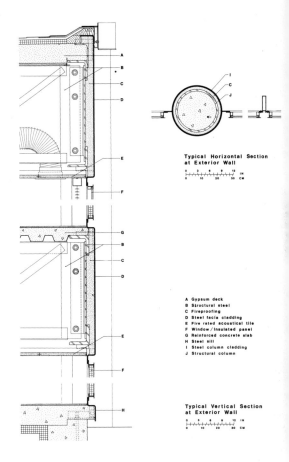

Typical Horizontal Section
at Exterior Wall

A Gypsum deck
B Structural steel
C Fireproofing
D Steel facia cladding
E Fire rated acoustical tile
F Window / Insulated panel
G Reinforced concrete slab
H Steel sill
I Steel column cladding
J Structural column

Typical Vertical Section
at Exterior Wall

246–253

The Wendell Smith Elementary School,
Gately Park, Chicago, 1972–73,
by Arthur Takeuchi, Chicago.

Elevation and section of the building, horizontal
and vertical detail sections.

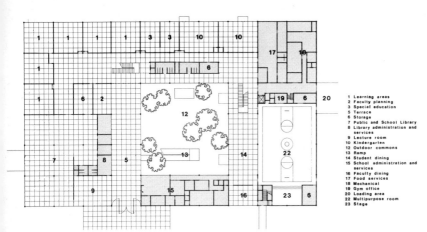

First Floor Closed Plan

```
0    20   40   60    FT
0       10      20    M
```

1 Learning areas
2 Faculty planning
3 Special education
5 Terrace
6 Storage
7 Public and School Library
8 Library administration and
   services
9 Lecture room
10 Kindergarten
12 Outdoor commons
13 Ramp
14 Student dining
15 School administration and
   services
16 Faculty dining
17 Food services
18 Mechanical
19 Gym office
20 Loading area
22 Multipurpose room
23 Stage

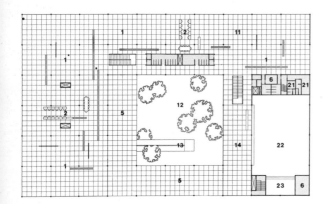

Second Floor Open Plan

```
0    20   40   60    FT
0       10      20    M
```

1 Learning area
2 Faculty planning
5 Terrace
6 Storage
11 Science laboratory
12 Outdoor commons
13 Ramp
14 Student dining
21 Staff lockers
22 Multipurpose room
23 Stage

248

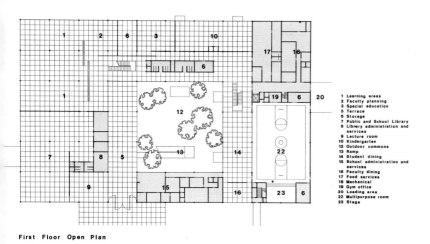

First Floor Open Plan

```
0    20   40   60      FT
0        10       20   M
```

1 Learning areas
2 Faculty planning
3 Special education
5 Terrace
6 Storage
7 Public and School Library
8 Library administration and
  services
9 Lecture room
10 Kindergarten
12 Outdoor commons
13 Ramp
14 Student dining
15 School administration and
   services
16 Faculty dining
17 Food services
18 Mechanical
19 Gym office
20 Loading area
22 Multipurpose room
23 Stage

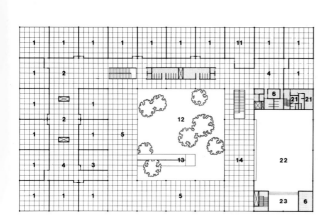

Second Floor Closed Plan

```
0    20   40   60      FT
0        10       20   M
```

1 Learning areas
2 Faculty planning
3 Special education
4 Corridor learning areas
5 Terrace
6 Storage
11 Science laboratory
12 Outdoor commons
13 Ramp
14 Student dining
21 Staff lockers
22 Multipurpose room
23 Stage

Plans of the building.

249

Study of materials and color with the aid of a model. The steel skeleton is painted white and the interior rooms in color (not executed).
251

Open space and playground terrace on the upper floor.

The black of the skeleton construction is matched
to the environment. The courtyard with its open
grid pattern is surrounded by the building on all
sides.

Roberto Clemente High School, Chicago,
by Dirk Lohan, 1973–74

General considerations
The great fire of 1871 which largely destroyed the
downtown area of Chicago was the occasion for a
large-scale reconstruction on a city-wide basis. But
Chicago can also look back upon a progressive tradition of school building which began as long ago
as the late 19th century. Since Mies died in 1969
the architectural office has been continued by his
partners and long-standing collaborators Joseph
Fujikawa, Bruno P. Conterato and Dirk Lohan
and is accommodated in its own building on the
top floor of the One Illinois Center (1969–72).
Since mid-1975 this office has operated under the
new name FCL 'Fujikawa Conterato Lohan and
Associates'. Dirk Lohan, previously partner-in-
charge of the former Office of Mies van der Rohe,
is responsible for school-building projects. The
clear expression of the skeleton construction has
also survived in the new partnership. 'Nevertheless
we cannot stand still where Mies stopped or we
run the risk of stagnating', said Dirk Lohan.

Spatial organization
The nine-story building of the Roberto Clemente
High School for 3000 pupils is located in the north-
west of Chicago. Interior access is by a pair of esca-
lators and two elevators. The detached sports hall
is also used by the public.

Technical development and aesthetic considerations
The concrete-sheeted steel skeleton has a square
column grid with a lateral dimension of 30-foot
bays. Between the columns there is an infill of
light-colored brickwork or steel windows with relatively small divisions. The columns are painted
matt black and are flush with the infill of the skeleton. An elegant steel bridge of truss girders two
stories high spans the 130 feet between the sports
center and the school building.

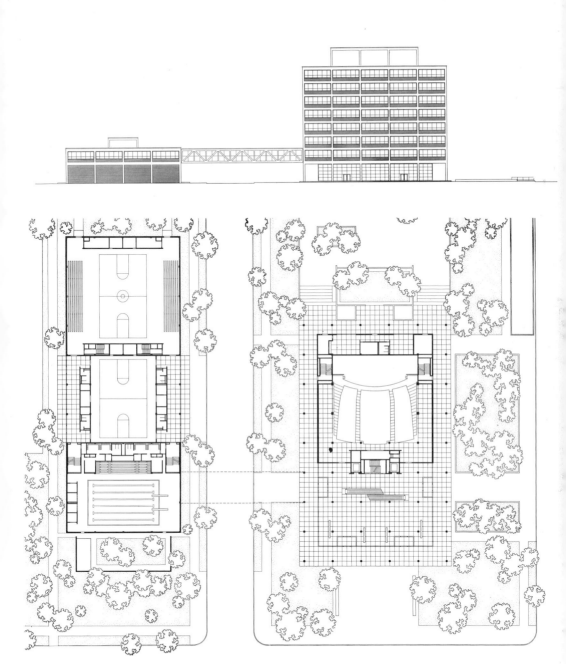

254–259

Roberto Clemente High School,
West Division Street, Chicago, 1973–74.
Architect-in-charge Dirk Lohan
(The Office of Mies van der Rohe, Chicago, now
FCL = Fujikawa Conterato Lohan and Asso-
ciates, Chicago).

General plan with 9-story classroom block and
2-story sports center.

255

The classroom block and sports center are joined
by a steel bridge of trussed girders. Ceiling height
about 9 feet. The buildings are air-conditioned.
257

Columns and beams in matt black, infill of light-colored brickwork.

Multistory Office Building at Elkhart (Indiana),
by Myron Goldsmith, 1972-74

General considerations
Myron Goldsmith is one of the most active of
Mies' successors. He worked on important projects
in Mies' office and is today a partner with SOM
and also a professor at IIT. He mainly advises
students working on large scale projects leading to
their master's degree.
In recent years these theses have been an inspira-
tion to architecture. It might be said that many
large buildings can be traced back to these thesis
projects at ITT. As a creative architect and animat-
ing spirit at IIT Myron Goldsmith holds a very important position in which his training as an engineer and architect stands him in good stead.

Spatial organization
In the small mid-west town of Elkhart this modest
5-floor building of the St. Joseph Valley Bank, the
first building in the newly developed commercial
center, shows how the character of the school of
Mies can be given expression by means of subtle
precision in independent designs based on structural development and the open-plan system.

Technical development and aesthetic considerations
A steel skeleton frame with wide spans and broad
openings. The facades are sheathed in aluminum
painted white. Transparent glass was used for the
windows. Sun protection is provided by inside curtains. A spiral stairway leads from the wide space
of the banking hall down to the vaults in the basement. This stairway, probably the most spectacular
feature in the building, is of incomparable beauty
and simplicity. The elegance of the stairs and the
restraint in the pattern of the facade as a contrast to
the rhythmical skeleton structure are characteristic
of the engineer architect. The clear structure is
reflected in the delicate lines of the facade details.

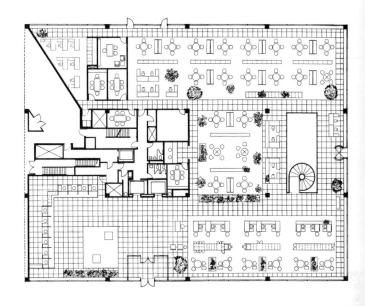

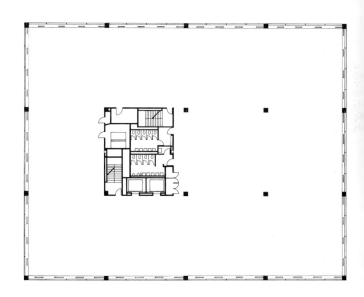

260–267

Multistory Office Building at Elkhart (Indiana),
1972–74. Architect-in-charge Myron Goldsmith
(Skidmore, Owings & Merrill, Chicago).

Ground-floor plan of the St. Joseph Valley Bank
and typical floor plan.

261

Steel-and-glass facade with 40-foot intervals between the columns.

Unity of structure and form. The work of an engineer architect.
265

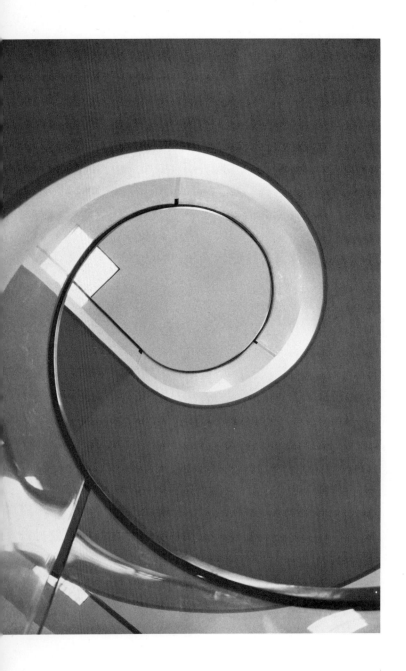

The circular stairway leading to the lower level is a
striking freestanding steel structure imbedded in
concrete.

88 Pine Street Office Building, New York,
by James Ingo Freed, 1972–74

General considerations
My examples come almost exclusively from Chicago. This limitation was a help to me in tracing the records embodying Mies' principles on the scene of his activity. James Ingo Freed, who emigrated from Germany and Switzerland, worked on the Seagram Building, and was trained at IIT, is an architect who has realized the ideas of Mies outside Chicago.

Spatial organization
This 32-story office tower occupying a site 216×94 feet and with a large plaza in front of the building is located in Lower Manhattan on Wall Street: it faces the East River. With its lucid skeleton system and large areas of glazing this building may also be said to be a product of Mies' Chicago school.

Technical development and aesthetic considerations
The Orient Overseas tower office block (88 Pine Street Office Building) was the recipient of the R. S. Reynolds Memorial Award in 1974. The cheaper aluminum facade is based on a rather more expensive steel facade. That is why I have shown here the first design as well as the version actually built. The facade cladding in white aluminum is more strongly accented as befits the material. The columns are spaced 27 feet apart. The 7 fields between columns on the fronts and the 3 fields on the sides ensure great flexibility.

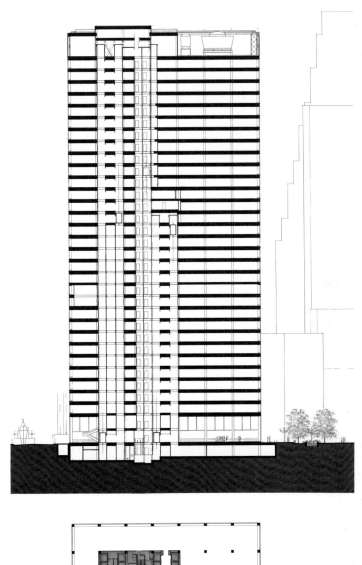

268–273

Office Building 88 Pine Street (Lower Manhattan),
New York, 1972–74.
Architect-in-charge James Ingo Freed
(I. M. Pei & Partners, New York).

Plan and section through the 32-floor building.

Subtle detailing of the aluminum cladding. The
facade detail of the school of Mies set a trend.

The steel skeleton is fireproofed with concrete and faced externally with white aluminum panels. The metal outer skin is an expression of the structural function.

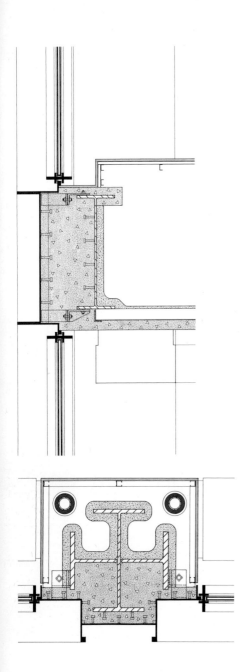
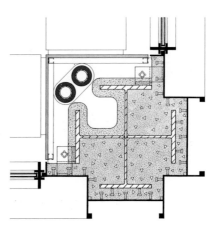

Vertical and horizontal section of the first version
with steel sheath (not executed).

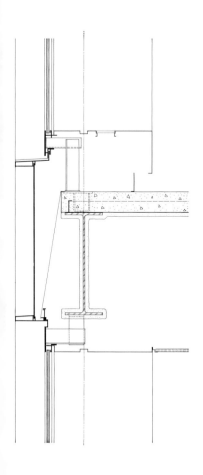

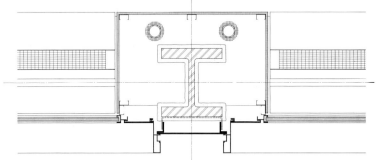

Horizontal and vertical section of the final design
in aluminum.

Auraria Higher Education Center, Denver
(Colorado), General Plan
by Jacques C. Brownson, 1973–76,
library by Helmut Jahn (C. F. Murphy Assoc.)

General considerations
In downtown Denver a new college for the State of
Colorado to accommodate 30,000 students is in the
course of construction. Jacques C. Brownson, who
has often figured in this book, has since 1973 been
putting into operation a plan in which the ideal
column grid pattern (30-foot bays) affords maximum flexibility. Here is an opportunity to imple-
ment Mies' idea that the skeleton remains unal-
tered but that functions can change in the course of
time. Understandably then, the detailing of the
facade must be subordinated to the structure.
Brownson maintains that it is immaterial whether
the walls are executed in brick or in light building
elements. The design grid that applies to the whole
area remains of paramount importance.

Technical development
Helmut Jahn of C. F. Murphy Assoc. wrapped a
skin of aluminum and glass round the building of
the Auraria library which has round concrete
columns like every other building on the campus.
Brise-soleils were installed on the glass skin to afford
protection from the glare of the sun. In the interior
the building services are installed where they can
be seen so that spatial alterations are possible at
any time.

Aesthetic considerations
The library with its white baked enamel aluminum
facade is a foil to the dark earth-colored brick
buildings on the campus. Planted patios in the interior give the building variety. The internal space
is an open system in which Miesian detail in the
broadest sense can be applied. The teaching of
Mies is basically unchanging but, as the illustrations show, it can expand and develop.

274–279

Auraria Higher Education Center,
Denver (Colorado), 1973–76.
Master plan: Jacques C. Brownson.
Library: Architect-in-charge Helmut Jahn
(C.F. Murphy Assoc., Chicago).

Site plan of campus.

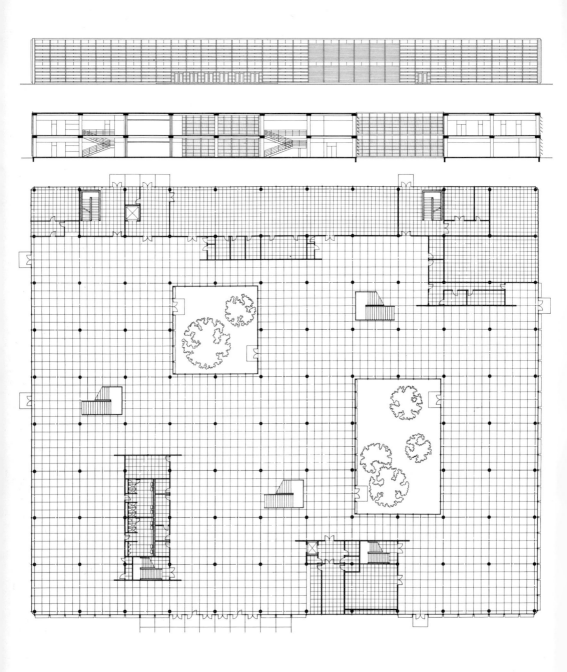

The skeleton system permits space to be devoted to
a variety of functions. The technical development
is visible and aesthetically integrated.

Plan and elevation scale ca. $\frac{1}{60}'' = 1'0''$.

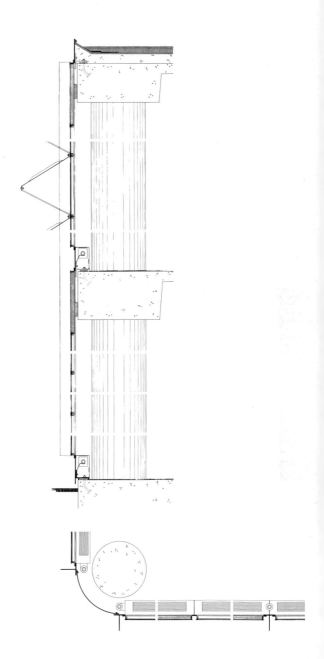

Horizontal and vertical section through curtain
wall (steel).
277

Facade with brise-soleil elements.
279

Homage to Walter Gropius
by Ludwig Mies van der Rohe,
Chicago, July 29, 1969

It was a kindness of fortune that allowed Walter
Gropius, so near the end of his life, to be present in
Stuttgart at the opening of the 50-year anniversary
exhibition of the Bauhaus – the school he founded
which embodied one of the most vital ideas for education in our epoch.
As I look back over the 60 years I have known him,
as one of the leading architects of our time, and the
greatest educator in his field, I am struck by his
generosity of spirit.
The divisive forces in this century have been
powerful – disorder, competitiveness, specializa-
tion, materialism. This condition never discour-
aged Gropius from seeking unity in diversity. It
never undermined his conviction that people could
work more fruitfully in collaboration than in com-
petition. It never shook his courage in pursuing a
course of coordinating and integrating the efforts
of many. He had the rare talent for bringing people
together.
As I said of him years ago, he was always a gallant
fighter in the never-ending battle for new ideas. His
participation in this battle endured to the end of a
long and productive life.
These are, in my opinion, Gropius' noblest legacies
to all of us.

(The very last thing Mies ever wrote, only three
weeks before he died.)

Acknowledgments and thanks

A conversation in my Basle office in 1972 with
George Danforth, the successor of Mies van der
Rohe as head of the Department of Architecture at
IIT (1959–75) and subsequently with his partner,
Daniel Brenner, strengthened me in my intention
to bring out for the younger generation of architects a book with its main emphasis on the principles Mies taught at IIT. Together with my long-
standing collaborator Ernest Persche, a graduate of
IIT, I produced the first version of the exposé on
the principles and school of Mies and its sequel.
I undertook my first journey for research purposes
to Chicago in autumn 1972. On that occasion I
filled out my draft of the book together with the
successors and personal friends of Mies. I gave
priority of attention to models of educational value
and buildings which are of particular interest
today. On my journey to Chicago in May 1976,
when my purpose was to check the text and illustrations, I first visited Denver in Colorado. There I
met Jacques C. Brownson, an ex-student of Mies,
who has been planning a campus for 30,000
students since 1973. His plan is based on a 30-foot
bay extending over the whole area. This made it
possible for various architects to work at different
sites at the same time and for the facade design to
vary from building to building.
Back in Chicago I was aware that the teaching of
Mies will develop a further stage under James Ingo
Freed, the new dean and at the same time head of
the Department of Architecture. The present generation at IIT, which has multiplied in numbers
since Mies' day, is making a great effort to achieve
further progress. Mies' Crown Hall is also used
as a workshop for work on models and plans.
I realized, too, that Mies' teaching had also developed outside Chicago. Alfred Caldwell, one of the
most fundamental interpreters of Mies, is propa-
gating Mies' principle of the unity of material,
structure and space by the example of his own
house, for which he used erratic blocks from the
nearby stream.
I am particularly grateful to the team in Chicago
whose friendship I have enjoyed for many years:
Myron Goldsmith, Ogden Hannaford, Dirk Lohan,
Lora Marx and Arthur Takeuchi. I am also in-
debted to Ludwig Glaeser from the Mies van der
Rohe Archive at the Museum of Modern Art in
New York for access to drawings (Robert McCormick House). My thanks are likewise due to Pro-
fessors Bernhard Hoesli, Paul Hofer and Alfred
Roth of the Board of Trustees of the 'gta' (Institute
for the History and Theory of Architecture at the
Swiss Federal Institute of Technology in Zurich)
and to Christina Reble, editorial secretary, for
valuable suggestions.
Two monographs in which the work of Mies van
der Rohe is presented – Oswald W. Grube '100
Years of Architecture in Chicago', Munich 1972
and Chicago 1976 and Peter Carter 'Mies van der
Rohe at work', 1974; David Spaeth favorable

Bibliography on Mies, Lexington (Kentucky),
1980 – are valuable supplements to my own work.
Mies died in Chicago in 1969 but his school and his
work live on.
His literary and artistic remains are in the custody
of the 'Mies van der Rohe Archive' at the Museum
of Modern Art in New York and are accessible to
the public.

Note on the second edition

This expanded English-language edition of the
book originally published in America under the
title of 'After Mies', underlines three factors arising
in the present 'Chicago School of Architecture'
which will be important for the coming decade.
The first of these three factors is that for the first
time since Mies a European, Gerald R. McShef-
frey, has been in charge of the Department of Architecture, the Department of City and Regional
Planning and the Institute of Design at IIT since
1979 as Dean of the College of Architecture, Planning and Design. With the appointment of George
Schipporeit, a former pupil and assistant of Mies,
as Chairman of the Department of Architecture in
1980, the heritage of Mies was assured.
Second, there is talk again at IIT of the importance
of the teaching of Professor Alfred Caldwell as architect, landscape architect, planner, poet and
philosopher; he worked with Mies van der Rohe,
Ludwig Hilberseimer and Walter Peterhans for fifteen years. Actually, Mies wanted him as his successor in 1959, but he left IIT in protest because
Mies could not complete his campus project there.
Extract from an IIT report: 'The teacher architect
Alfred Caldwell taught students to build. As a
builder he knew materials first hand and came to
understand their nature and possibilities in building. His courses were eloquent demonstrations of
principle and idea, and of the great fundamentals
of structure, scale, proportion, order and harmony.
He saw – and the students learned to see – the
detail in the whole and the whole as more than the
sum of the parts – Organic Architecture. In his lectures he demonstrated that beauty cannot be
sought for its own sake. That beauty is a consequence of the inner nature of things. He would
demonstrate how span affects structure as it in-
creases from a few feet to a thousand feet. He
showed how architecture was related to its time yet
demonstrated new possibilities – future change. As
a teacher he was a leader, guide, and more than little a tyrant. He was also informed and Socratic and
demanded by his own example that students give
their best to the work. His history lectures were
more than history. Strongly philosophical in con-
tent they enabled the student to think clearly about
the nature of architecture.

A Town House in Chicago (Kenwood 54th Street)
David Hovey 1977–79

General considerations
David Hovey distinguished himself while still a
student of Arthur Takeuchi at IIT with the collage
on the book jacket. From the architect himself:
Later while working with C.F. Murphy (today
Murphy/Jahn) in the mid-70's I became increas-
ingly interested in a slightly different approach to
the traditional architect, owner, contractor relationship and decided to focus especially on the housing
industry where architects seem to have had little
positive effect in America.

Spatial organization
With the Optima Simplex six-unit project, which
was completed in 1979, Optima Inc. was able to
purchase the land, design, construct and market all
within fifteen months. It is my hope to eliminate
the middle man where possible and employ modern industrial techniques of construction to achieve
cost savings which can be passed on to the owner in
better accommodations and equipment. These
three-story single-family urban residential units are
located in the heart of Hyde Park. Each contains
three bedrooms, two baths, recreation/family
room, utility room and private garden.

Technical development
Construction is of brick bearing-walls and precast
concrete floors and roof. Principal habitable rooms
face south; this is also the more private side of the
site. Large windows are located on the south side to
take advantage of the solar heat during the winter
months. Retractable fabric sunshades provide
shade in the summer. The north public street elevation consists of smaller windows to insure isolation
from noise and to provide privacy. Voids in the
precast concrete are used in lieu of sheet metal
ducts to distribute air for heating and cooling.

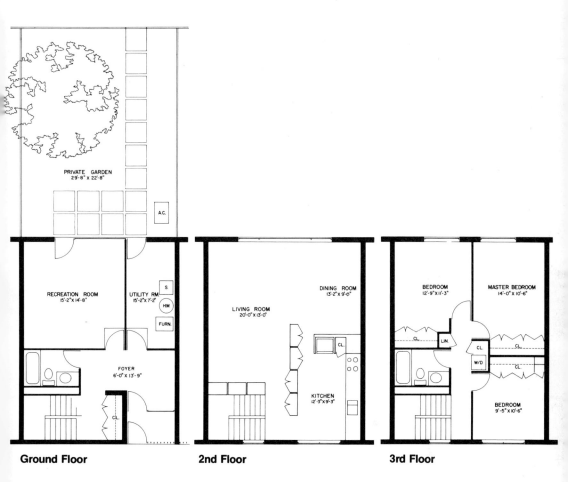

Ground Floor

PRIVATE GARDEN
29'-8" X 22'-8"

A.C.

RECREATION ROOM
15'-2" x 14'-8"

UTILITY RM.
15'-2" x 7'-2"

S.

HW

FURN.

FOYER
6'-0" X 13'-9"

CL.

2nd Floor

DINING ROOM
13'-2" X 9'-0"

LIVING ROOM
20'-0" X 13'-0"

CL.

KITCHEN
12'-3" X 9'-3"

3rd Floor

BEDROOM
12'-9" X 11'-3"

MASTER BEDROOM
14'-0" X 10'-6"

CL.

LIN.

CL.

CL.

W/D

CL.

BEDROOM
9'-5" X 10'-6"

TYPICAL FLOOR PLANS

Typical floor plans.

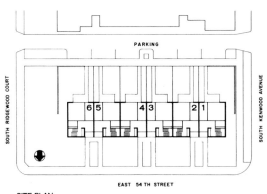

PARKING

SOUTH RIDGEWOOD COURT

SOUTH KENWOOD AVENUE

6 5 4 3 2 1

EAST 54 TH STREET

SITE PLAN

Integration of material and structure with the environment.

Maywood Garden House (High-Rise Apts. project)
Forest and River Oaks (Illinois)
George Schipporeit 1977

General considerations
Thoughts by the architect: A phase of housing architecture has attempted to develop more of an internal community concept by orienting the apartments around a central vertical atrium. The first concern was to improve the security of inner city high-rise buildings by being able to see across the atrium and have the surveillance of people moving about. This function was reinforced even more by its application to housing for the elderly and the experience of seeing people bring their chairs out to sit by the atrium and watch the world go by. About 1,500 units are completed or presently under construction which incorporate this atrium orientation with various mutations.

Aesthetic considerations
Garden House has been planned as both a dignified home and a personalized neighborhood. The atrium open space at each level gives the typical corridor a sidewalk feeling. The walk home among neighbors creates friendliness and security by having visual surveillance. The entrance door can now be left open as an invitation for someone to drop by.
To achieve more of an individual identity for each dwelling the corridor wall has been recessed approximately two feet to provide a separate cove of lighting and color. The solid core oak door continues the theme of the wood atrium railing, and the wood railing provides for random placement of planting boxes to add both flowers and hanging ivy to create a sense of nature.

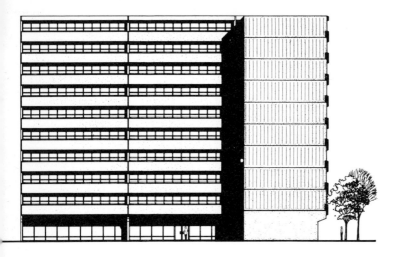

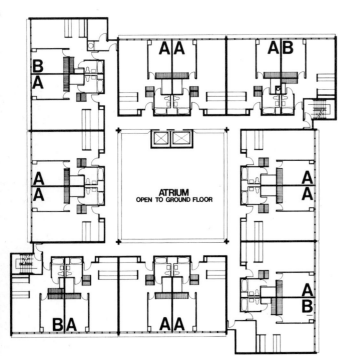

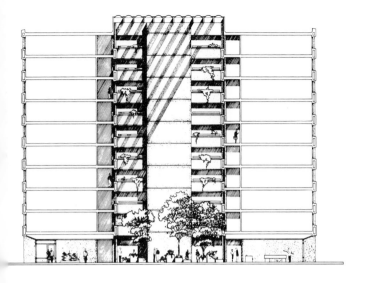

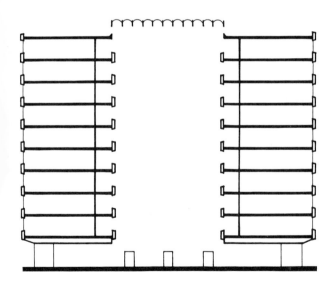

The atrium becomes the scene of year-round activity. Section and front elevation.

Ruck-A-Chucky, a hanging arc bridge, Auburn
California T.Y. Lin International, Hanson En-
gineers, San Francisco, Architectural Consultant
Myron Goldsmith, SOM Chicago, 1976

General considerations
The Ruck-A-Chucky Bridge will cross the Middle
Fork, American River, over the Auburn Reservoir,
with a singular curved span of 1300 ft. The horizontal arc flows into the hillsides, and the steepness
of the slopes is utilized to support the entire span.
This unique design will indeed enhance the environment and will add to the scenic beauty that sur-
rounds the area.

Technical development and aesthetic considerations
The recommended structure by the design team:
'After considering and comparing over a dozen
bridge types which might be constructed to cross
this canyon, we have finally developed a "Hanging
Arc" concept which clearly appears to be the most
appropriate solution. This structure fits into the environment with simplicity, economy and elegance.
The horizontal arc allows the bridge to flow into
the hillsides, minimizing the heavy approach cuts
at both ends. The unusual steepness of the neighboring slopes is turned into an asset by utilizing
them, in place of costly towers, to suspend the entire span. Indeed, here nature furnished us with
provisions for multiple cable supports, a most
favourable arrangement to hang an arc bridge and
a good way to reduce the depth of the bridge deck.
The absence of water-submerged piers solves the
difficulty of resisting hydro-seismic forces, which
are formidable in deep waters subjected to earth-
quakes. Totally suspended from the mountains
above, this defiant but delicate ribbon will not only
remain undisturbed by fluctuating water levels, but
will enhance the scenery of the lake with its changing reflections.'

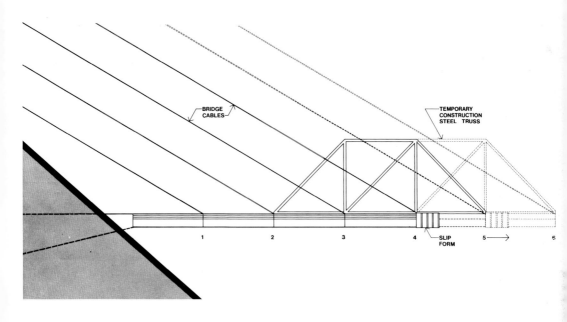

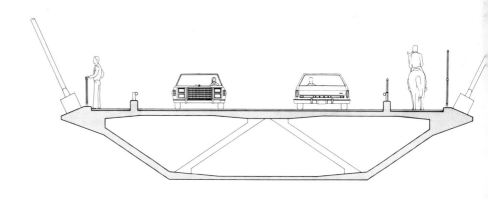

Ruck-A-Chucky Bridge Auburn Dam, construction sequence.

A spectacular bridge for the canyon of the American River. The sketch of the ground view shows the bridge hanging from the sides of the canyon.

State of Illinois Center, Chicago 1979 –
Principal-in-charge Helmut Jahn
Project Architect James Goettsch
Architect/Engineers Murphy/Jahn
Joint Venture Architects Lester B. Knight, Inc.

Urban planning
The State of Illinois Center in downtown Chicago
is a government office building which is presently
under construction. The architectural team: 'The
south-east portion of the block is sliced away to
form a sloped, setback configuration and open the
space at the corner in response to the Searborn-
Clark Corridor, the City/County Building and the
Civic Center, without losing the spatial closure of
the street. The continuous but stepped-back west
façade of the building rises from the street line to
reinforce the LaSalle Street Canyon. An indenta-
tion of the skin at the lowest two floors creates a
covered arcade which continues along both LaSalle
and Clark Streets as well as along the curved south-
east wall. The arcade provides a zone of spatial
transition into the Rotunda. Along Randolph and
Clark, the granite screenwall of the arcade continues to define the open space, but diminishes gradually in deference to the entry. The plaza thus
created is a free composition of water, paving and
trees. The Lake Street elevation is a straight wall
along the building line which gives a clear reading
of the setbacks on the other exposures.

Spatial organisation
The building is a statement of the importance and
dignity of state government. This language empha-
sizes an appropriate scale and urban monumentali-
ty for a government building. The truncated glass
cylinder projects above the building mass, creates a
top and makes a clearly identifiable statement on
the skyline of the city. There is an appropriate sym-
bolic reference to the centrality of government and
to the prototype of domed government buildings
throughout the history of the building arts. The
new element in the State of Illinois Center is the
reading of the central space from the outside. This
element of openness is continued along the curved
façade by the five-story atriums which follow the
setbacks.

Aesthetic considerations
The abstract form of the building derives its meaning from conceptual, historic and urban references
and from their synthesis with today's materials and
techniques. This synthesis of many influences sur-
passes any attempt to use geometry or historical
references as the generator for form in Architecture. A glazed skin encloses all surfaces of the
building in a 2'-6" vertical division. Opaque
glasses, colored blue-grey-white, are used with sil-
ver and clear glass to create various levels of trans-
parency and reflections and give the monumental
shape a painted quality on the surface.'

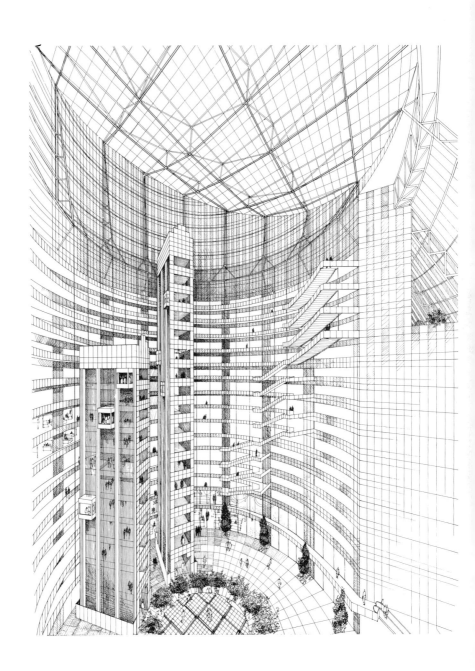

The elevation study of arcade columns seeking to
enclose the landscaped plaza.

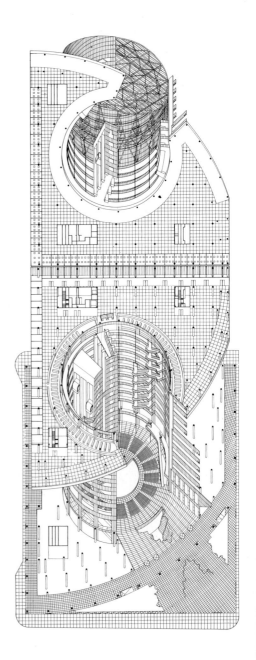

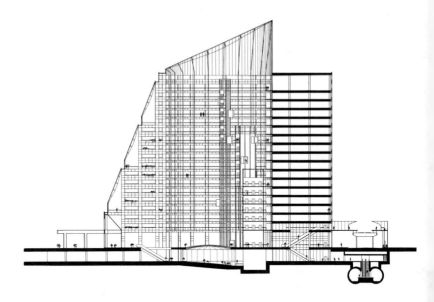

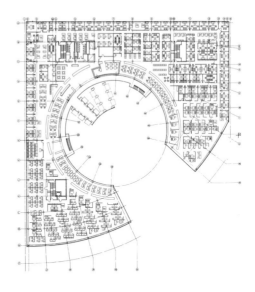

Drawing studies of the tall, clear glass building are
both a symbol and an invitation.

The building, with a huge central atrium, will be a ringing declaration of the State's presence in downtown Chicago.

Some books from Mies' library

The complete contents of Mies' personal library have been
excellently cataloged by Richard Seidel. These books are
in the custody of the Department of Special Collections, the
Library, University of Illinois at Chicago Circle. In 1975,
at my request, members of Mies' family, and a close
friend (with whom he often read) identified the following
titles as the ones most important to Mies. In 1952, Mies
told students at the School of Design of the North Carolina State College that he owned 3000 books in Germany
and that he had brought 300 with him to America. Of
these he could have sent back 270. He would not, he said,
have discovered the remaining thirty unless he had read the
3000 books. It is in this light that this list of some of his
books (collection in the possession of the family) should
be considered.

Adler, Mortimer J.
    The Difference of Man
    and the Difference It Makes.
    Holt, Rinehart and Winston, 1967.

Ardrey, Robert
    The Territorial Imperative, Atheneum,
    New York 1966.
    African Genesis, Dell, New York 1961.

Aristoteles
    Über die Seele. Übertragen von Adolf Lasson.
    Eugen Diederichs, Jena 1924.

Aristotle
    The Student's Oxford Aristotle, Politics
    and Poetics.
    Oxford University Press, 1942.

Aquinas, Thomas
    The Basic Writings of Thomas Aquinas.
    Edited by Anton C. Pegis.
    Random House, New York 1945.

Blaser, Werner
    Tempel und Teehaus in Japan, Otto Walter
    Verlag, Olten 1955.

Berlage, H. P.
    Studies over Bouwkunst, Styl en Samenleving.
    W. L. and J. Brusse te Rotterdam, 1910.
    Grundlagen und Entwicklung der Architektur.
    W. L. and J. Brusse, n. d.

Bieber, Margarete
    The Greek and Roman Theater.
    Princeton University Press, 1961.

Bohr, Niels
    Atomic Physics and Human Knowledge.
    John Wiley & Sons, New York 1958.

Bronowski, J.
    Science and Human Values.
    Julian Messner, New York 1956.

Burger, Fritz
    Die Villen des Palladio.
    Bayrische Akademie der Wissenschaften.
    Herausgegeben von Klinkhardt & Biermann,
    Leipzig 1909.

Boetticher, Karl
    Die Tektonik der Hellenen.
    F. Riegel, Potsdam 1852.

Buytendijk, F.J.J.
    Erziehung zur Demut.
    A. Henn Verlag, Ratingen 1962.

Cali, François
    Das Gesetz der Gotik. Prestel Verlag, München
    1963.
    L'Ordre grec, essai sur le temple dorique.
    Photographies de Serge Moulnier.
    Arthaud, Paris 1958.
    Architecture of truth.
    G. Braziller, New York 1957.

Teilhard de Chardin, Pierre
    The Future of Man. Harper & Row,
    New York 1964.

Confucius
    Gespräche. E. Diederichs, Jena 1921.

Chamberlain, Houston Stewart 1855-1927
    Die Grundlagen des neunzehnten Jahrhunderts.
    F. Bruckmann, München 1909. 2 volumes.

Condit, Carl W.
    The Rise of the Skyscraper.
    The University of Chicago Press, 1952.

Cornford, F. M.
    Principium Sapientiae,
    The Origins of Greek Philosophical Thought.
    Cambridge University Press, 1952.
    The Unwritten Philosophy
    and Other Essays.
    Cambridge University Press, 1950.

Le Corbusier
    Aircraft. The Studio Publications Inc., 1935.

Dessauer, Friedrich
    Philosophie der Technik.
    Friedrich Cohen, Bonn 1927.

Dornbusch, Charles
    Pennsylvania German Barns.
    Schlechter's, Allentown, Pennsylvania 1958.

Dreuermann, Fritz
    Naturerkenntnis. Volume 6 of Das Weltbild.
    Herausgegeben von Hans Prinzhorn,
    Müller & Kiepenheuer, Verlag, Potsdam 1928.

Durm, Josef
    Die Baukunst der Griechen.
    Alfred Kroner Verlag 1910.

Eddington, A.S.
    Die Naturwissenschaft auf neuen Bahnen.
    Friedrich Viehweg, Braunschweig 1935.
    The Expanding Universe. Ann Arbor Paperbacks,
    1958.

Einstein, Albert
    Ideas and Opinions. Crown, New York 1954.
    Out of my later years.
    Philosophical Library, New York 1950.

Eiseley, Loren
    (the anthropologist and historian of the University
    of Pennsylvania)
    The Mind as Nature. Harper & Row, New York
    1962.
    (The John Dewey Society Lectureship, 5.)
    The Immense Journey, Random House, New York
    1957.
    Darwin's Century, Doubleday, New York 1968.
    The Firmament of Time. Atheneum, New York
    1966.
    Francis Bacon and the Modern Dilemma. Lincoln,
    Neb.,
    University of Nebraska Press, 1962.

Egdell, G.H.
  The American Architecture of Today.
  Charles Scribner's Sons, 1928.

Eucken, Rudolph
  Die Lebensanschauungen der grossen Denker.
  Leipzig 1912.

Fischer, Theodor
  2 Vorträge über Proportionen.
  Oldenburg Verlag, 1934.

Fitchen, John
  The Construction of Gothic Cathedrals.
  Oxford at the Clarendon Press, 1961.

Francé, Raoul F.
  Der Weg zu mir.
  Alfred Kroner-Verlag, Leipzig 1927.
  Streifzüge im Wassertropfen.
  Kosmos-Verlag, Stuttgart 1906.

Freyer, Hans:
  Theorie des gegenwärtigen Zeitalters.
  Deutsche Verlagsanstalt, Stuttgart 1958.

Fuchs, Eduard:
  Illustrierte Sittengeschichte.
  Verlag Albert Langen, München 1912 (Privatdruck).
  3 volumes. Ergänzungsbände.

Gebser, Hans
  Abendländische Wandlung.
  Ullstein, Frankfurt a. M. 1960.

Ghiselin, Brewster
  The Creative Process. A Mentor Book, 1952.

Gilson, Etienne
  Being and Some Philosophers. Pontifical
  Institute of Medieval Studies, Toronto 1949.

Gotshalk, D.W.
  Art and the Social Order.
  University of Chicago Press, 1947.

Gleichen-Russwurm, A. von
  Die gotische Welt.
  Verlag Julius Hoffmann, 1919.

Goodyear, William Henry
  Greek Refinements, Studies in
  Temperamental Architecture.
  The Yale University Press, 1912.

Grohmann, Will
  Paul Klee. W. Kohlhammer, Stuttgart 1954.

Guardini, Romano
  Über das Wesen des Kunstwerkes.
  Rainer Wunderlich-Verlag, Tübingen 1959.

Hartmann, Nicolai
  Das Problem des geistigen Seins.
  Verlag Walter Gruyter & Co., Berlin 19, 1933.

Heidegger, Martin
  Kant und das Problem der Metaphysik.
  Verlag Diederich Cohen, Bonn 1929.

Hertz, Richard
  Man on a Rock. Chapel Hill,
  The University of North Carolina Press, 1946.

Hitchcock and Johnson
  The International Style: Architecture Since 1922.
  W.W. Norton & Company, 1932.

Hoffer, Eric
  The True Believer. New American Library,

New York 1963.
  The Temper of Our Times.
  Harper & Row, New York 1967.

Hoyle, Fred
  The Nature of the Universe.
  Harper & Brothers, New York 1950.

Hutchins, Robert M.
  The University of Utopia.
  The University of Chicago Press, 1953.

Huxley, Aldous
  Ends and Means. Harper & Brothers, 1937.

Huxley, Julian
  Evolution, The Modern Synthesis.
  Harper & Brothers, New York 1942.
  New bottles for new wine. Harper, New York 1957.

Jaeger, Werner
  Paideia: The Ideals of Greek Culture.
  Volume I: Archaic Greece, The Mind of Athens.
  Oxford University Press, 1945.

Jefferson, Thomas
  Life and Selected Writings of Thomas Jefferson.
  Edited by Adrienne Koch and William Peden.
  The Modern Library, 1944.

Kahler, Heinz
  Wandlungen der antiken Form.
  Münchner Verlag, 1949.

Kapp, Reginald O.
  Towards a Unified Cosmology.
  Basic Books, New York 1960.

Kant, Immanuel
  Kritik der reinen Vernunft.
  Insel Verlag, 1922.

Kerler, Dietrich Heinrich
  Weltwille und Wertwille.
  Alfred Kroner Verlag, 1925.

Boeke, Kees
  Cosmic View, the universe in 40 jumps.
  J. Day, New York 1957.

Kiesler, Frederick
  Inside the Endless House.
  Simon and Schuster, 1964.

Klopher, Paul
  Von Palladio bis Schinkel.
  Paul Neff Verlag, 1911.

Kung Futse
  Gespräche. Diederichs, Jena 1921.

Lerner, Max
  The Age of Overkill. Simon and Schuster,
  New York 1962.

Lorenz, Konrad
  On Aggression. Harcourt, Brace-World,
  New York 1966.

Lowe, Victor, Hartshorne, Charles and Johnson, A.H.
  Whitehead and The Modern World. Beacon Press,
  Boston 1950.

Mann, Thomas
  Last Essays. Alfred A. Knopf, New York 1959.

Maritain, Jacques
  The Range of Reason.
  Charles Scribner's Sons, New York 1953.
  The Rights of Man and Natural Law.

Charles Scribner's Sons, 1943.
Philosophy of Nature.
Philosophical Library, New York 1951.
An Introduction to Philosophy.
Sheed & Ward, Inc. n. d.

Mossel, Ernst
Vom Geheimnis der Form
und der Urform des Seins.
Deutsche Verlagsanstalt, 1938.

Munitz, Milton K.
Theories of the Universe.
The Free Press, Glencoe, Illinois 1957.

Nef, John
Bridges of Human Understanding.
University Publishers, New York 1964.
A Search for Civilization. Regnery, 1962.
The United States and Civilization.
The University of Chicago Press, 1942.

Novalis
The Novices of Sais. Illustrations with
60 drawings by Paul Klee.
C. Valentin, New York 1949.

Oppenheimer, F. Robert
The Open Mind. 8 lectures (and others).
Simon & Schuster, New York 1955.

Oparin, A. I.
The Origin of Life. Dover Publications,
New York 1938 (1953).

Ortega y Gasset, Jose (1883–1955)
The Origin of Philosophy. W. W. Norton,
New York 1967.
What is Philosophy? W. W. Norton,
New York 1960.
On Love. World Publishing Co.,
Cleveland 1963.
The Dehumanization of Art
(other writings on art and culture).
Doubleday, Garden City, N. Y. 1956.
Invertebrate Spain. W. W. Norton,
New York 1937.
History as a System. W. W. Norton,
New York 1961.
The Modern Theme. Harper & Brothers,
New York 1961.
Man & People. W. W. Norton,
New York 1957.
Man and Crisis. W. W. Norton,
New York 1962.

Panofsky, Erwin
Gothic Architecture and Scholasticism.
The Archabbey Press, 1951.

Prevost, Jean
Eiffel. Les Editions Rieder, 1929.

Price, Lucien
Dialogues of Alfred North Whitehead.
An Atlantic Monthly Press Book,
Little Brown and Company, Boston 1954.

Riehl, Alois
Philosophie der Gegenwart. Leipzig 1908.

Rodin, Auguste
Cathedrals of France. Beacon Press, 1965.
Original Publication, 1914.

Rourke, Constance
The Roots of American Culture.

Harcourt, Brace & Company, New York 1942.

Runes, Dagobert D.
The Dictionary of Philosophy.
Philosophical Library, New York 1942.

Russell, Bertrand
Authority and the Individual.
Beacon Press, Boston 1949.
Bertrand Russell's Best.
Selected by Robert Egner. Mentor Book, 1958.
The Scientific Outlook.
The Norton Library, 1931 (1959).

Smith, Huston
The Religions of Man. Harper & Row,
New York 1958.

Stahl, Fritz (pseud.) Karl Friedrich Schinkel
Schinkel-Monographie.
E. Wasmuth, Berlin 1912.

Scheler, Max
Die Wissensformen und die Gesellschaft,
Problem einer Soziologie des Wissens.
Der Neue Geistes-Verlag, Leipzig 1926.

Schneer, Cecil J.
The Search for Order.
Harper & Brothers, 1960.

Schopenhauer, Arthur
Sämtliche Werke in 5 Bänden.
Insel Verlag, n. d.

Schrödinger, Erwin
What is Life? And other scientific
Essays. Doubleday, Garden City, N. Y. 1956.
Was ist Leben? Die lebende Zelle mit
den Augen eines Physikers betrachtet.
L. Lehne-Verlag, München 1951.
Nature of the Greeks.
Cambridge University Press, 1954.
My View of the World.
The University Press, Cambridge 1964.
Mind and Matter.
Cambridge University Press, 1958.
Science and Humanism, Physics in our Time.
Cambridge University Press, 1952.

Schwarz, Rudolf
The Church Incarnate, the sacred
function of Christian architecture.
Henry Regnery Co., Chicago 1958
(Mies helped very much with
the translation – that is, he helped
Cynthia Harris to understand Schwarz's ideas).
Von der Bebauung der Erde.
Verlag Lambert Schneider, Heidelberg, 1949.
Vom Bau der Kirche. Heidelberg, 1947.
Wegweisung der Technik.
Aachener Werkbücher. Band 1.

Semper, Gottfried
Der Stil. Friedrich Bruckmann's Verlag,
München 1878. 2 volumes.

Shapley, Harlow
Of Stars and Men, The Human Response
to an Expanding Universe.
Beacon Press, Boston 1958.

Sullivan, Louis H.
The Autobiography of an Idea.
Press of the A. I. A., New York 1924.

Sun Tzu
The Art of War. Translated by
Samuel B. Griffith.
Oxford at the Clarendon Press, 1963.

St. Augustine
The City of God, London:
J. M. Dent & Sons Ltd., New York.
First published edition 1931.
E. P. Dutton & Co. Ltd.

St. Thomas Aquinas 1225–1274
The Basic Writings of Th. Aquinas.
Edited by Anton C. Pegis.
Random House, New York 1945.

Tax, Sol
Evolution after Darwin. 3 volumes.
Volume I: The Evolution of Life.
Volume II: The Evolution of Man.
Volume III: Issues in Evolution.
The University of Chicago,
Centennial Discussions, 1960.

Thompson, D'Arcy
Of Growth and Form. University Press,
Cambridge 1945.

Thoreau, Henry
Walden and other Writings.
The Modern Library, New York 1937.

Toynbee, Arnold J., ed.
Greek historical thought from Homer
to the age of Heraclitus.
New American Library, New York 1964.

Van der Velde, Henry
Geschichte meines Lebens. Piper, 1962.

Von Simson, Otto
The Gothic Cathedral. Bollingen Series,
Second Edition, 1962.

Waley, Arthur
Yuan Mei, Eighteenth Century
Chinese Poet.
George Allen and Unwin Ltd.,
London 1956.

Weiss, Paul
The World of Art. Southern Illinois
University Press, 1961.

Weizsäcker, C. F. v.
The Relevance of Science, Creation
and Cosmology.
Collins, London 1964.
The History of Nature.
The University of Chicago Press, 1949.
Die Tragweite der Wissenschaft. Volume I.
S. Hirzel Verlag, Stuttgart 1966.
Zum Weltbild der Physik.
S. Hirzel Verlag, Stuttgart 1963.
The World View of Physics.
University of Chicago Press (1949), 1952.

Werkbund. Jahrbuch 1913
Die Kunst in Industrie und Handel.
Jahrbuch 1914: Der Verkehr.

Weyl, Hermann
Symmetrie.
Princeton University Press, 1952.

Whitehead, Alfred North
Dialogues of Alfred North as recorded
by Lucien Price.
Little Brown, Boston 1954.
Adventures of Ideas.
Macmillan, New York 1947.
Science and the modern world.
The New American Library, New York 1948.

Whyte, Lancelot Law
Aspects of Form, A Symposium on Form
in Nature and Art.
Pellegrini & Cudahy, New York 1951.

Ziegler, Leopold
Florentinische Introduktion.
Felix Meiner Verlag, Leipzig 1912.
Zwischen Mensch und Wirtschaft.
Otto Reichl Verlag, 1927.

Some writings by Mies 1937–69

1937   Program for architectural education (p. 26–27)
1938   Inaugural address as director of Architecture at
        Armour Institute of Technology, Chicago
        (p. 28–30)
1940   Frank Lloyd Wright. An appreciation written for
        the unpublished catalog of the F.L. Wright
        Exhibition held at the Museum of Modern Art
        (College Art Journal No.6 1946)
1943   A Museum for a Small City (Architectural Forum
        No.65 1943.)
1944   Introduction: The New City by Ludwig Hilbers-
        eimer (Paul Theobald & Company Chicago 1944)
1950   Address to Illinois Institute of Technology (Philip
        Johnson, Mies van der Rohe, Museum of Modern
        Art New York 1953)
1955   Writings in Perspecta 3, The Yale Architectural
        Journal (p. 96–97)
1956   Letter to the Opening Ceremony of Crown Hall.
        (Philip Johnson, Mies van der Rohe, Verlag Gerd
        Hatje Stuttgart 1956)
1960   Address on the occasion of the presentation of the
        Gold Medal of the American Institute of Archi-
        tects at the Annual Convention in San Francisco
1963   Introduction to the Rudolf Schwarz Memorial
        Exhibition. (Akademie der Künste Berlin 1963)
1965   Walter Peterhans Visual Training Course at the
        Architectural Department of IIT (p. 34–35)
1969   Homage to Walter Gropius (p. 280)

Index

Bibliography

Blake, Peter
Mies van der Rohe – Architecture and Structure, Pelican
	Books, Baltimore 1960.
Blaser, Werner und Burckhardt, Lucius
Objektive Architektur – Mies van der Rohe. Werk, Bern,
	November 1964.
Blaser, Werner
Mies van der Rohe – Die Kunst der Struktur. Verlag für
	Architektur, Zürich 1965.
Blaser, Werner
Mies van der Rohe. Praeger Publishers, New York 1972,
	and A.D.A. Edita, Tokyo 1976.
Blaser, Werner
Il design di Mies van der Rohe, Electa Editrice Milano
	1980
Bonta, J. P.
Mies van der Rohe, Barcelona 1929. Editional Gustavo
	Gili S.A., Barcelona 1975.
Carter, Peter
Mies van der Rohe. Architectural Design, London, March
	1961.
Carter, Peter
Mies van der Rohe at work. Phaidon Press Limited Pub-
	lishers, London 1974.
Condit, Carl W.
The Chicago School of Architecture 1875–1925. The Uni-
	versity of Chicago Press, 1963.
Drexler, Arthur
Ludwig Mies van der Rohe. George Braziller Inc., New
	York 1960.
Glaeser, Ludwig
Ludwig Mies van der Rohe. The Museum of Modern Art,
	New York 1969.
Grube, Oswald W.
100 Jahre Architektur in Chicago. Die Neue Sammlung,
	München 1973.
Grube, Oswald W., Pran, Peter C. and Schulze Franz
100 Years of Architecture in Chicago. Museum of Con-
	temporary Art, Chicago 1976.
Hilberseimer, Ludwig
Mies van der Rohe. Paul Theobald Publisher, Chicago
	1956.
Hilberseimer, Ludwig
Die Entfaltung einer Planungsidee. Verlag Ullstein, Berlin
	1963.
Johnson, Philip C.
Mies van der Rohe. The Museum of Modern Art New
	York, 1947, and Verlag Gert Hatje, Stuttgart 1956.
Persitz, Alexander
L'œuvre de Mies van der Rohe. L'Architecture d'au-
	jourd'hui, Paris, septembre 1958.
Speyer, James
Ludwig Mies van der Rohe. The Art Institute of Chicago,
	1968, and Akademie der Künste, Berlin 1968.
Wingler, Hans M.
Das Bauhaus 1919–1933. Rasch-Verlag, Bramsche 1962.
	Kleine Bauhaus-Fibel, Bauhaus-Archiv-Verlag,
	Berlin 1974.
Spaeth, David
Mies van der Rohe – Bibliography, Garland Publishing
	Inc. New York 1980
Württembergischer Kunstverein:
	50 Jahre Bauhaus, 1968, und Supplement 1969,
	Stuttgart.

IIT Record and Mies Office Employment

Chronological list of some names cited in the text and
other collaborators (arranged by year of IIT degree,
teaching or employment in the Office of Mies)

Name	IIT degree	IIT faculty record	Office of Mies
Ludwig Mies van der Rohe		1938–58 Prof. and Dir.	1938–69
Ludwig Hilberseimer		1938–67 Prof.	(Planning consultant)
Walter Peterhans		1938–60 Prof.	
John Barney Rodgers	(Bauhaus)	1938–42 Assoc. Prof.	1938–42
William Priestley	(Bauhaus)	1940–42 Assoc. Prof.	1938–42
Howard B. Dearstyne	(Bauhaus)	1957–69 Assoc. Prof.	
A. James Speyer	1939 MS Arch.	1946–61 Prof.	
George E. Danforth	1940 BS Arch.	1941–53, 59–75 Prof. and Dir.	1939–44
James W. Hammond	1942 BS Arch.		
Charles B. Genther	(1939–43)		1945 (and Pace Assoc.)
William E. Dunlap	1947 BS Arch.	1949–51 Instr.	1948–50
R. Ogden Hannaford	1947 BS Arch.	1960– Assoc. Prof.	1950–54
Bruno Conterato	1948 BS Arch.		1948–75 (partner '69)
Alfred Caldwell	1948 MS CP	1945–60 Prof.	(Landscape consultant)
Reginald Malcolmson	1949 MS Arch.	1949–64 Assoc. Prof.	1948–49
Daniel Brenner	1949 MS Arch.	1949– Prof.	1947–52
Edward Duckett	(1944–50)	1945–46 Asst.	1944–65
Gene R. Summers	1951 MS Arch.		1950–66
Yau Chun Wong	1951 MS Arch.	1974–75 Assoc. Prof.	1950–58
Myron Goldsmith	1953 MS Arch.	1961– Prof.	1946–53
Joseph Fujikawa	1953 MS Arch.		1943–75 (partner '69)
David Haid	1953 MS Arch.		1953–59
Jacques C. Brownson	1954 MS Arch.	1949–59 Asst. Prof.	1948–50
James Ingo Freed	1953 BS Arch.	1975–77 Prof. Dean	1955–56
Pao Chi Chang	1954 MS Arch.	1973– Asst. Prof.	1953–59
Henry Kanazawa	1954 MS Arch.		1953–58
Yujiro Miwa	1954 MS Arch.		
Peter Roesch	1956 MS Arch.		
George Shipporeit	(1955–57)	1980– Chairman Arch.	1957–60
Peter Carter	1958 MS Arch.		1958–71
Louis J. Johnson	1958 MS Arch.	1962– Assoc. Prof.	1958–62
Conrad Roland	1958 MS Arch.		1958–61
Dirk Lohan	(1957–58)		1962–75 (partner '69)
Arthur S. Takeuchi	1959 MS Arch.	1965– Asoc. Prof.	
Paul A. Thomas	1961 MS CRP	1958– Assoc. Prof.	
Erdmann Schmocker	1961 MS Arch.	1965– Assoc. Prof.	
David Carold Sharpe	1962 MS Arch.	1962– Assoc. Prof.	1958–60
Phyllis Lambert	1962 MS Arch.		1960
Jong Soung Kimm	1964 MS Arch.	1966– Assoc. Prof.	1961–72
John Carl Heinrich	1965 B Arch.	1972– Asst. Prof.	
Fazlur Khan, Ph.D.	(U. Illinois)	1966– Adj. Prof.	
Paul A. Zorr	1967 MS Arch.	1969– Asst. Prof.	1963
Peter C. Pran	1969 MS Arch.		1963–66
Alfred T. Swenson	1968 MS Arch.	1966– Asst. Prof.	
Robin L. Hodgkinson	1968 MS Arch.		
Helmut Jahn	(1966–68)		
Ernest Persche	1969 B Arch.		
Dennis P. Korchek	1972 MS Arch.	1975– Asst. Prof.	1968–71
Terry Young	1972 B Arch.	1975– Instr.	1967–72
Rimantas Pencyla	1972 MS CRP	1970–73 Instr.	
Peter Beltemacci	1965 MS CRP	1980– Chairman CRP	
San Utsonomyia		1980– Asst. Dean	
Gerald R. McSheffrey		1979– Prof. Dean	
Dale Fahnstrom		1980– Chairman I.D.